MAKING
good

MAKING good

AN INSPIRATIONAL GUIDE TO BEING AN ARTIST CRAFTSMAN

JACKLYN SCOTT | KRISTIN MÜLLER | TOMMY SIMPSON
Foreword by Stuart Kestenbaum

Schiffer Publishing Ltd

4880 Lower Valley Road • Atglen, PA 19310

Contents

Foreword

For the profiles in *Making Good,* Kristin Müller and Jacklyn Scott interviewed forty-one makers, asking them about their work and the experiences that have shaped it. You'll notice that I made it through the first sentence of this foreword without using the words "craft" or "art." That's because I find that sometimes defining "craft" can make people uncomfortable. Well, maybe more often than sometimes. Where does craft end and art begin? Is it brown and itchy? Can I charge more for it if I give it another name? As much as I love the subtleties of language, words can be used to reinforce status and hierarchy. Even people who work in craft may want to back away from that particular word from time to time to fit in with the larger and more powerful art world.

I feel most comfortable bypassing the conversation altogether and talking about makers and creativity. But last year, as I was preparing to leave my job as director of the Haystack Mountain School of Crafts after twenty-seven years, I was asked to be on a call-in program on public radio in Maine.

Since "craft" sits right in Haystack's full name, on the way to the station, I found myself thinking that certainly someone would ask me to define craft, and there I would be, on the air, staring at a microphone, and required to give an answer. As anyone involved in a creative enterprise knows, there is nothing like a deadline to focus your attention, so driving along Route 15 from Deer Isle to Bangor, the definition came to me.

Craft consists of three elements: knowledge, skill, and intuition. It's a relationship among these parts, and the three need each other. They balance and they adjust. They learn how to talk to each other and listen.

It's this balance that you will find in *Making Good.* Knowledge is history: remembering those who came before, connecting generations of ingenious humans. Skill is the practice: it's the time spent teaching the hand to move the right way or having the hand teach the brain to see, or both. It calls for tenacity. Then comes intuition, the wild card in the creative process.

You're in your studio. You know your history. You probably have inspirational images from the past tacked to your wall. Your tools are there, tools that you have grown so comfortable with that they are extensions of your body. Your material—wood, clay, metal, glass—is your partner in the process. Your skill and knowledge are a deep part of you that moves through your body like unconscious thought, like your autonomous nervous system. Then there comes a gesture, a mark, a decision, when your intuition kicks in. Or perhaps leaps forward. This is when the maker (painter, jeweler, potter, poet, glassblower, blacksmith, woodworker, weaver, designer…) comes to life. And when the maker comes to life, the work can too. And isn't that what we are after? Whatever we choose to call it, it can speak for itself.

Stuart Kestenbaum

Introduction

Tommy Simpson and I have known each other for more than twenty years. We met at the Brookfield Craft Center when he enrolled in my weekly pottery class. I remember vividly how he looked up from the potter's wheel and admitted that his pottery teacher had been Mia Groettell when I wasn't even born yet. I took a deep breath to calm my nerves because I was just a little intimidated to be teaching one of the most prolific artist craftsmen of our time. His authentic curiosity and desire to make soon gave way to a deep friendship and several opportunities to collaborate on exhibitions and making work. The first time my daughter, Jacklyn Scott, met Tommy she was nine years old. Her impression was "Mom, Tommy looks like he was struck by lightning." I have never forgotten how precise her observation was. Tommy has been blessed, possessed, and touched by a profound talent and drive to create. He often collaborates with artists who work in different media to expand his own capacity to create. Perhaps the most amazing quality Tommy has is his generosity and kindness. This is a man who feels so lucky to practice his art that he wants others to know the joy.

Tommy, Jacklyn Scott, and I share such a love of making that we want others to know this, too. This is how the three of us came together to work on this book—partially because we really enjoy each other and mostly because we represent three generations of artist makers who love what we do and have met great people along our personal journeys. Our hope is that this book will provide authentic insight into what it takes to make a career as an artist and most of all what it means to live the life of an artist, craftsman, designer, or maker.

The individuals we have chosen to represent in this volume are only a fraction of the artists whose work we deeply admire. Of course, we had to set some parameters to reach a consensus of whom we could include. We worked hard to represent artists in a wide range of craft media because that is the world we know best. We worked toward covering the geographic range of the United States but admit we have more artists based in the east because it is where we have most of our networks. We chose to limit the number of people we included who earn their living by being full-time professors, since there are many other ways artists assemble their lives to support themselves through their work. We purposely selected some artists who have worked in the field for less than ten years, and some who have worked in the field for more than thirty years, along with those in between. We believe you will see clearly in these pages the confidence embodied by those who have succeeded, the confidence that is building for midcareer artists who have begun to see a clear path, and the questions and mystery that lie ahead for those who are just beginning.

As we interviewed each artist we discovered that some artists make for art's sake, finding ways to earn a living only in other ways. Others are keenly focused on earning a living with their art and making work that responds to the market. Most artists figure out a way to balance the conundrum between the exploration of new ideas and the discipline to complete the necessary work to make a living. There really is no one way to approach the life of a maker. And each approach has its own advantages and drawbacks. When reading this book you will find a synthesis of the character of each individual, how they came to choose the life of an artist, what challenges and lucky breaks have helped shape their careers, what they have sacrificed to succeed, where they are in their life pursuit, and some of the ways they have responded to key opportunities that led fruitfully to the next ones.

Here we attempt to authentically present the lives of makers through their own voices and work. Each artist has a website or gallery listed where you can look up their résumé. We believe that it is more important to feature the stories that aren't represented in a curriculum vitae. That's the humanity and personality behind the work.

We are very grateful to each of the artists who agreed to participate and opened their hearts to share pivotal moments in their lives. They shared their vulnerability, ambitions, failures, and successes with honesty and intimacy. The conversations we had with each artist are a gift to us. In sharing their gorgeous work and stories, we hope that you will be inspired to explore the potential you hold within.

The most challenging part has been to accurately distill the passion, challenges, opportunities, drive, and introspection that define each of their individual practices in a succinct and effective way, ultimately presenting how artists put their soul into their work to make a good life and make good in the world.

Kristin Müller

A life's pursuit of building with your hands centers around the creative making of objects imbued with insight and beauty. This quest into the arts is a path that leads toward finding one's unique voice. It offers the artist greater understanding of being alive, and, with a little bit of luck and persistence, being creative hopefully provides the artist with a living.

The purpose of this book is to provide a helpful guide collected from the experiences of like-minded makers. These individuals represent a mixture of genders, ages, backgrounds, and inclinations. In their own words they tell us about their journeys to become artists.

My own history started in America's heartland, the great Midwest, full of family farms and artisans. In my youth, I remember answers to "how to" problems were resolved by asking a friend or neighbor. Their experienced remedies to my incessant curiosity came from a lifetime of hands-on problem solving passed from generation to generation. This hand-to-hand exchange of information widened my understanding of problem solving and broadened my worldview.

I became a maker of objects and ideas.

My life in the arts has given me the opportunity to put my heart on the line, and to bring to life the elements needed to be creative and useful. If granted a wish, I would ask that all beings have the same opportunity to find themselves, and to bring their inner life to actuality.

Tommy Simpson

Garry Knox Bennett

Wood

gkb-furniture.com

Quite early on in life, Garry Knox Bennett knew he liked art. A teacher had told him that his penmanship was so beautiful that he should think about pursuing art professionally, and he did. Garry studied painting at the California College of Arts and Crafts in Oakland, California, where he gained a strong education in academic art. After college, he married his wife, Sylvia, and moved out to the country to live simply and paint. "We spent many years being very poor, but I kept painting. I always wanted to be a painter. When we were living out there, I was smoking a lot of the magic product and I realized that I needed a better way to hold it, so I started making roach clips." Garry would bring them to local recording studios, and they would pass them on to clients like The Beatles and The Rolling Stones.

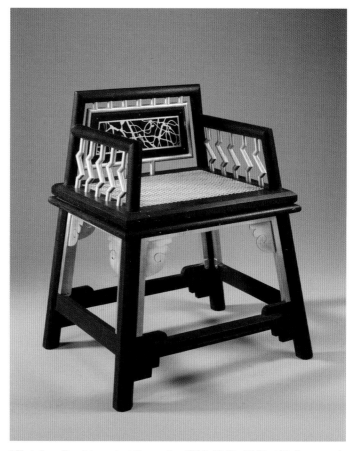

"Chair for a Small Important Person" c. 2005, 28.5" x 22.5" x 19". Rosewood, matte 23k gold-plated copper and brass, inlaid nautilus shell.

After moving back to Oakland, Garry continued producing intricate and beautiful roach clips as well as peace symbol necklaces that he could easy produce with a limited amount of tools and space. This bread and butter business allowed him the resources to get back into making his art work. Garry decided to explore the possibilities of making clocks. He had very few woodworking tools, but he had a lot of metal tools, so he made clocks out of mostly metals with wood accents. "The wood part was primitive but I liked it and what I could do with wood to make something large." Garry had access to a plating company, so he could employ plated metal elements into his furniture as well.

Julie's Artisan Gallery, in Manhattan, invited Garry to exhibit his series of clocks, each like a small-scale sculpture employing various media to give depth and context to the work. He also started showing with Snyderman-Works, American Craft Museum, and Franklin Parrasch Gallery. After connecting with Leo Kaplan

"All of the great people who supported us are dying off. We need someone with a lot of money and influence over the youth of today to start buying art. It would be a real renaissance."

"Lamp" c. 2009, 17"×20"×5". Rosewood, timber bamboo, polished aluminum, oxidized copper-plated brass, paint.

Modern and Peter Joseph Gallery, Garry decided that he was a furniture maker. "I realize that I'm not a very good painter, but I am a very good furniture maker. I paint because I love it. I do it when I get tired of building, and I'm getting older and weaker so I'm working much smaller now." Garry says that it was a great time to be a furniture maker in the 1980s. At any exhibition he put on, almost everything would sell, and sometimes he would get commissions from it. Garry gained notoriety for his iconic "Nail Cabinet" in 1979 after driving a nail into the front of a rare wood cabinet he had built to perfection. Most furniture makers at the

Garry in the studio at the band saw.

Exhibition (partial view) with "Eames Wall-Chair" set, two "Chair Paintings," and an early sideboard/buffet, "That Jackson, He Spits!"

"Altar Table" c. 2005, 35"×88"×21". Rosewood, timber bamboo, polished aluminum, oxidized copper-plated brass, paint.

Exhibition (partial view) with five of Garry's "electro-prints," two of his chair paintings, a coffee table with underpainted glass top, "Dirty Lipstick" bench, "Twirling Lamp," and assorted chairs.

time were still building brown furniture, but Garry would include various elements, including plated metals, glass, and bright paints. "I had no compunction about painting wood, even really good wood, which freaked people out."

Galleries are closing due to the high costs of rent in cities. Garry says that his sales have slowed because shipping costs are so high that it's impossible to send work to be shown on the East Coast. "The West Coast has never been good for sales for me, but I still sell with Gallery NAGA in Boston."

Garry continues to live and produce work in his studio in Oakland, California, with his wife, Sylvia. He occasionally temporarily employs assistants to help with the sanding of larger pieces. Garry spends six to eight months painting, because it brings him joy.

Dixie Biggs has been a full-time woodturner and artist since 1989. She has had an extensive show career and exhibited her work in such notable venues as the Smithsonian Craft Show, Philadelphia Museum of Art Craft Show, and del Mano Gallery. She has shared her techniques and knowledge at various woodturning clubs, symposia, and craft schools around the country.

"I can't remember a time when I wasn't fascinated with working with wood. My mother enjoyed carving, but put it aside after having children. Apparently, as a toddler, I would get so close watching that she was afraid she was going to cut one or the other of us. According to her, I got my first pocketknife at about kindergarten age. It was a much earlier age then she would have liked. My interest in woodturning began in 1979 when I taught myself to use a wood lathe so I could duplicate a chess set my grandfather had made. Although I'm primarily self-taught, I've had some great advice and inspiration from many other wood-turners and artists along the way."

Dixie Biggs

Wood
dixiebiggs.com

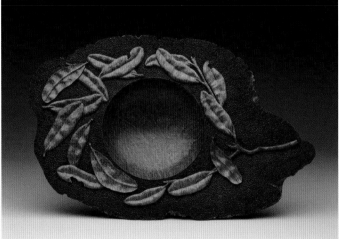

Photo credit: Randy Batista

"Southern Exposure" c. 2008, 2"×14"×9". Brown mallee burl. Turned, carved, and wood burned.

Having a degree in agriculture and a love of the outdoors, Dixie incorporates a botanical theme in much her work, and finds inspiration in the shapes, textures, and simple beauty found in nature. Her sculptural pieces create a restful place for her turned work, and they provide the sense of tranquility that a quiet walk in the woods can bring. "I always wanted to be an artist. I always like creating with my hands and then looking back at the end of the day and seeing what you've accomplished."

"On the Fence" c. 2009,
25"×10". Cherry turned
and then carved.

"Natural History" c. 2006, 5.5" × 5". Cherry turned and then carved.

"I experience a great deal of excitement watching a piece take shape from my hands. I never know what I'm going to find once I get below the bark of a log. Sometimes there is buried treasure! It is such a thrill when I find unexpected swirls, burls, patterns, and colors. I love finding wood that others have discarded and breathing new life into it. I feel I've accomplished this when someone can't resist picking up a piece of my work and caressing it."

Like many artists, Dixie let her fear of public speaking stop her from opportunities to teach and share her knowledge with others. When she turned fifty, she promised herself a change. "At some point in time, I was asked to do a major demonstration. I did it on my fiftieth birthday. I decided that the second fifty years of my life are going to be different than the first fifty. I told myself, 'I'm going to get over this fear.' And once I did that, it opened a lot of doors for me as far as demonstrating and teaching at schools, like Peters Valley School of Craft, Arrowmont School of Arts and Crafts, and John C. Campbell Folk School."

"Lip Service" c. 2010, 5.5"×7"×5". Cherry, pyrography, and acrylic paint. Turned, carved, wood burned, and painted.

"SereniTEA" c. 2013, 5.25"×6.5"×5". Bleached ash, ebony, and boxwood with maple rake. Turned and then carved.

"Early on, there weren't as many women in woodworking. My stubborn part said 'I can do this and I can do it better.' I had a desire to prove that I could do it."

At the lathe.

"Sakura" c. 2014, 6"×11"×5.5". Cherry, pyrography, and acrylic paint. Turned, carved, wood burned, and painted.

Dixie's success is not short of sweat and labor. She bought her property, built her own house, and built her own shop. "I've never had to have a mortgage, so as I saved money, I would put it into the house. I don't feel like I've sacrificed a whole lot. I was just never afraid of hard work."

Lynda
Grace Black

Fibers

instagram.com/lyndagraceart

"Validation from my
artist friends told me
this is right for me
and I can do it. They
inspire me."

Lynda Grace Black is a fiber and mixed media artist who works full time as an executive assistant at La Salle University in Philadelphia. She learned how to knit and crochet primary stitches from her grandmother and aunt, and grew up knitting, but at some point early on, she put her needles and hooks down.

It wasn't until Lynda was in her thirties that she circled back to her grandmother for knitting and crochet refresher lessons. A turn of events that led to finding herself without a job provided her time for introspection, and that is when she began working with fiber once more, but this time with a renewed sense of commitment. Lynda candidly admits that making scarves and sweaters never interested her very much. Her grandmother's advice prompted her to continue learning by taking classes from an

"Item 2: Aspirations of the Lost, the Longing and the Ignored #17" c. 2015, 2.25"×2.5"×2.5". Tsumugi silk yarn, polyester yarn.

"Item 3: Aspirations of the Lost, the Longing and the Ignored #1" c. 2014, 3.5"×3"×2". Polyester yarn, hemp twine, brass.

"Item 1: Aspirations of the Lost, the Longing and the Ignored #27" c. 2015, 2"×3.25"×3". Bamboo yarn, sisal.

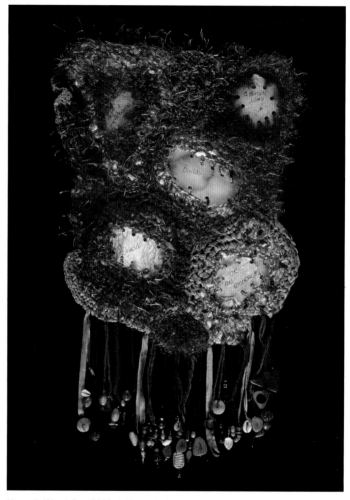

"Item 6: Words" c. 2002, 26"×15.25". Wool, acrylic, cotton, nylon, paper, ink, tea, wood, bone, shell, moose horn, metal, glass, tiger's eye, agate.

accomplished beading teacher at Fleisher Art Memorial in South Philadelphia, and joining the Bead Artist Collective, where she met other artists who were willing to share their skills with one another.

For Lynda, her choice to become an artist has been validated by the response to her work and encouragement from professional artists and attention from the media. Affirmation from her peers fuels her passion to pursue work. "Early on it was just doing the work. Then people began to tell me they see things in the work, they see some spirit in the work, something extremely valuable, and I thought, okay, you, there is something happening here, embrace it, go for it."

"Item 7: An Act of Love" c. 2002, 10.5"×8.25". Cotton, rayon, acrylic, silk, wool, shell, glass, bone, tiger's eye, garnet, freshwater pearl, metal, assorted beads.

Most of her work is sold work through exhibitions, commissions, craft fairs, and personal connections. Most recently her series "Aspirations of the Lost, the Longing and the Ignored," though seemingly gentle and delicate in material, is profoundly political and spiritual in content. This marked her transition from creating wearables to creating work with a more political message that prompts contemplation. Having a full-time job provides support for her lifestyle and the freedom to explore her work freely. The steady income provides her with a way to explore ideas intently without the pressures of the marketplace and lets her better focus on content and context.

Linda sitting at her studio table.

There is strong element of storytelling in her work that draws inspiration from artists such as El Anatsui, Ann Hamilton, Sheila Hicks, and Barbara Chase-Riboud. Most of Lynda's ideas come from observing people, social justice issues, and personal experiences or concerns.

"Barbara Chase-Riboud…helped me find a way to include profound personal stories in my work, so others might consider the untold stories in a world that sometimes says 'the single story' is the only story that defines how we interact with or judge people."

Having studied originally in the craft mediums, Nancy Blum's work in the public sphere employs materials, ideas, and methods based on her training as a ceramic sculptor. Nancy's public artwork also reflects the splendor of the natural world; she utilizes imagery of flora and fauna, mathematical progressions, and patterns that are reflective of far-ranging cultures. Her substantial experience with mixing materials (metal, mosaic, glass, ceramic, concrete) and varying art strategies (integrated, two- and three-dimensional, functional, free standing) enables her to create large-scale and public artwork for communities. While always contributing beauty to an environment, her work strikes a balance between sculptural permanence and ephemeral effects.

Nancy Blum

Wood

nancyblum.com
instagram.com/nancy_blum

Photo credit: Richard Nichole

"Hatch Covers: Fifty Hatch Covers for Seattle Arts Commission" c. 2001, 42" round. Cast iron.

"Some pieces sing. They have a rhythm and keep the eye active, and they draw people in and seduce the viewer, and some works just don't have that aliveness, and I can tell the difference, luckily."

Nancy spent countless hours drawing as a child, and still does. From as far back as she can remember, she had a desire to be an artist. In fact, when she was in third grade she told her camp counselor that she was going to be the first famous woman artist, because she thought there weren't any! As she approached applying to college she grappled with the idea that making art perhaps didn't contribute enough to the world, and she chose the path of social work instead. While pursuing her social work degrees she took electives in the art department to satisfy her need to keep creating art. After graduation she found herself without a studio, so she enrolled in art classes at local colleges to have access to fully equipped studios.

Because Nancy already had a master's degree in clinical social work and could support herself, she began to feel she could move

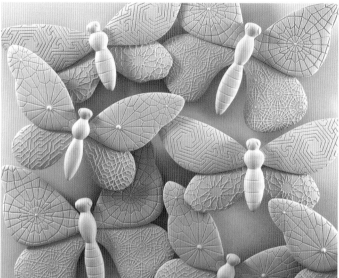

peach credit: Cathy Carver

"Butterflies" c. 2005, 12"×15"×2" each of ninety forms.

"I think that to work as an artist does intrinsically mean to live as an artist. It has to be a vocation in that way because it is uncharted."

in the direction of art as an occupation. Nancy was accepted into Cranbrook Academy of Art, where she earned an MFA in ceramics while maintaining a clinical practice. During her time there, with many studios and a culture for exploration, she also found herself immersed in metals, glass, concrete, and bronze casting. She took in as much technical and material knowledge as she could, further deepening her interest in combining craft materials.

Nancy recounts hearing the psychiatrist Elisabeth Kübler-Ross speak about how most people are too frightened to take action and don't have the confidence to believe that they will be provided for. Those words, the notion that everything will be okay, that you will be provided for, hit her like a bolt of lightning. The idea of shifting career paths was simmering deep down, but those words gave her the boost of confidence she needed to take the leap and commit to making a living as an artist. At that particular moment she realized that she had aspired to be an artist, but it was now time to accept that she *is* an artist.

After completing her MFA she completed an artist-in-residency program at the Archie Bray Foundation for the Ceramic Arts and then another at the Pilchuck School of Glass. She credits these opportunities to totally immerse herself in working for her own sake as critical to her professional pursuit.

"Residencies are often places where there is enough space and support to get to the core of what you want to do for yourself, not what other people find interesting."

"Entwine" c. 2011, 50"×122". Ink, colored pencil, gouache, and graphite drawing on paper.

"I think one of the ways to be an artist is just to force yourself to find a way to make a living doing it. You just take a leap. It doesn't happen any other way. You don't get the career first."

Nancy still struggled with the notion of art being enough of a contribution to the world, and began seeking out public art projects. From a philosophical perspective, public art projects have provided fulfillment of her ideals and values. Today, public art is an important component of her income stream, and she finds that it complements her design and drawing practice while also engaging her love of mixing media. Some of the pragmatic benefits are that public art works are longer working cycles, with larger budgets that facilitate collaboration between a variety of people in different professions, along with artists and fabricators. The scope and scale expands the possibilities for the studio artist.

Nancy has found a good balance to her artistic practice, which also includes large-scale botanical drawings she creates in her home studio. The studio is a fairly large room where drawing and model making are easily accommodated. For the fabrication of the public works she collaborates with studios and is able to work in glass, bronze, clay, concrete, and metal. In addition to being a full-time artist, she teaches workshops at craft schools and colleges, and she lectures.

"The thing I like about public art is that in many aspects it is a collaboration, and many aspects of it are design. I have an opportunity and I have to respond to that client or opportunity, and

Photo credit: Gene Ogami

"Trumpet and Passion/Harbinger" c. 2012. Ink, colored pencil, gouache, and graphite drawing on paper.

Photo credit: Jackie Brown

"Flower Wall (parts)." Resin and aluminum cast elements in studio waiting for assembly.

Drawing in the studio.

in that something new comes out. Even though it will look like it's mine, pulling on my ideas or expertise, it becomes something new."

At a young age, Dana Boussard remembers working on art projects alongside her artist mother. She describes her family as living artistic lives. Her mother was an avant-garde poet, and her father, a dentist by trade, was a talented musician. Dana and her sister played two instruments each and attended art lessons as early as age six. She always knew she would have an artistic career, but says she never imagined that she would go on to have the successful art career that she has today.

Dana majored in art at a Catholic women's college, but after two years she found that the religious atmosphere was not for her; she felt like a bit of a hippie. The school didn't offer the degree

Dana Boussard

Mixed Media /
Performance
danaboussard.com

Photo credit: Ariana Boussard-Reifel

"We Met with Oh Such Separate Dreams II" c. 2013, 53"×116". Cotton velvet, paint, painted fiber construction.

of life drawing training that she felt she needed, as it did not allow nudity. She transferred to the Art Institute of Chicago, double majoring in English and art. "It was fabulous! It really set the tone—it had a great reputation and everyone there was very serious and dedicated." Just before Dana graduated, her father became sick. A one-semester break from school turned into a year, at which point she packed up her apartment in Chicago and moved home to Montana. She took some courses at the University of Montana and soon, because she had been pursuing a double major, her advisors there told her she had enough credits for a BFA. She took a few more classes anyway, to keep her busy and in the studio.

"While I finished school, I got married. He was an amazing ceramist. I earned my MFA and we both moved forward as professional artists. We did very well for being so young." Dana realized that she wanted to work in a larger scale, but larger

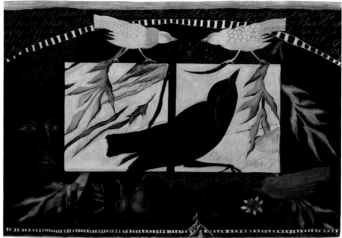

"Separation Anxiety" c. 2014, 30"×44". Mixed media on paper, drawn.

"I'm an artist because I don't have to work a set eight hours a day; I can work twelve hours a day whenever I want!"

pieces meant increased overhead. So she began working at an artisan school program in Great Fall, Montana, where students could observe her working. She soon divorced her first husband and invested her money earned from the artisan school job in a piece of land. Dana bought sixty acres in Missoula, Montana, with a barn and a one-bedroom log cabin. Her dad helped with the down payment for the house, but she invested all of her money into the property to make it into "a great little studio." Soon thereafter, Dana became restless and decided to move to New York City.

Stan Reifel, the executive director of Fairtree Gallery in New York City, had previously contacted Dana about featuring her work. A few weeks into living there, she decided to go to the gallery and introduce herself. "He was very excited to meet an artist whose work he had in the gallery. We fell in love very quickly, and well, the rest is history." Dana worked in her studio for about a year while busily applying for commissions.

Dana has built her career from more than sixty large-scale commissions varying in price from $2,000 to $350,000. Her first commission, in 1972, was to make a large hanging piece for the ceiling of the student center at the University of Oregon. She outsourced some of the work that she didn't have the capacity or skill to do herself, like cutting large scale Plexiglas and some of the woodworking. "When I was done, I realized that, yeah, it cost me money, but now I'm in the game."

Stan is an incredible asset to Dana, she says, due to his curatorial and museum crating experience, which helps Dana ship her work. For preparing a shipment, Dana was able to hire one or two

"And You Are the Branches" c. 2009/2015, 22"×6", 42"×8" 22"×6", three of eight windows. Holy Spirit Catholic Parish, Great Falls, Montana.

assistants, and Stan would build the crates and assist in transporting and installing the work. Dana says that having this support system really took away any of her fears about her ability. She knew that she could do anything and work at any scale.

Dana had applied for a job as a professor right out of graduate school, but realized that it was a full-time commitment that would take away from her studio practice. That was not something she was willing to do. "I am a studio artist; that's who I am. If I have to be poor all my life, then that's what I'll do."

Fortunately for Dana, she had very supportive parents in terms of finances, and she also received some money when her father passed away. She and Stan were smart in their investing choices, too.

> "To me, drawing is the most immediate and personal place to put your creativity."

The artist working on a stained glass installation in her studio. Arlee, Montana.

When Dana's husband, Stan, had a very serious stroke, she put all her work on hold for a few months until Stan was back on his feet. After Stan's stroke, Dana changed her work flow because she could no longer depend on Stan for the heavy lifting. She feels it has been good for her. She hopes to explore more performing and video art. Currently, she's working on a drawing commission for the cover of a book.

Growing up in a household of artists and creatives, it seemed only natural that Ariana Boussard-Reifel would follow in their footsteps. Her mother, Dana Boussard (also featured in this book), is an active studio artist; and her father, Stan Reifel, is a talented museum and gallery curator as well as a furniture maker. They raised Ariana to know how to work with her hands and use power tools. Growing up on a ranch in Montana, Ariana learned early on how to create worlds and keep herself entertained.

"A lot of my skills came from experimentation and watching my parents work. From a very young age, I was on the floor of my dad's shop gluing his scraps together to build cityscapes, or in my mom's studio painting." Ariana went to Carleton College and received her bachelor of arts in sculpture. She learned various technical skills in college, like metal fabrication, and various material studies. "My core materials are fragile and responsive. I use paper, wax, cloth, air, light, and language to mirror aspects of the human experience. Each of these humble materials is prone to change, evaporation, and disintegration. Paper yellows with

Ariana Boussard-Reifel

Mixed Media / Performance
arianaboussardreifel.com

"Between the Lines" c. 2007, 3.5"×10.5"×8". Transformed book.

"Manifest" c. 2014, 3.5"×10.5"×7.5". Transformed book.

Artist and her mother performing "Like Mother, Like Daughter."

"Litost, detail" c. 2006, 180"×10"×65". Mixed media.

"My parents and I share a craft…not just that we make things with our hands but that we make our lives by making things with our hands."

time, wax slumps with heat, much like language evolves under the influence of its era." Ariana moves through materials and ideas freely; she is not afraid of trying to achieve competency in all mediums.

When she first moved to New York, Ariana took an internship with a sculpture artist, fabricating metal structures. Taking a good look at her life, Ariana knew she needed to consider whether she wanted her art making as a means to her financial stability or if she needed to explore another source of income. She chose to enroll in a postbaccalaureate program at Virginia Commonwealth University, known for its prestigious sculpture program. At the end of her time there, Ariana realized that she enjoyed making as

The artist with Dana Boussard and Stan Reifel after installing their piece "Hate Begins at Home."

"Narcissian Columns" c. 2006, 12"×130"×100". Parrafin, paper.

a creative release, so she decided she would use her entrepreneurial spirit to find another way to support herself financially. "I still show my work aggressively and still make some of my income from my work, but it took a lot of the pressure off and made it possible to explore things I was interested in. The New York City art world is a social experience that you really have to participate in. I extricated myself from that, and it was an emotional and labored decision, but I'm very happy about it."

Because Ariana had an understanding of fabric from her mother, and because as a sculpture artist she was always looking for found objects to include in her art, it felt natural for her to launch a vintage clothing business. It grew into a profitable company selling vintage and antique jewelry as well as Ariana's own line of jewelry. Her company, Marteau, allows her to make small wearable sculptures as a more "commodifiable" way to put pieces of art out in the world. She continues to take classes in metalsmithing, and her work has shifted a great deal in the last six years.

Ariana's work was shown early on in her career at various galleries and museums, most notably at the Holter Museum of Art in Helena, Montana. Her work, especially her altered books, circulated via social media, resulting in collectors contacting her to purchase work. She continues to sell work through word of mouth, especially to book art collectors. That doesn't mean Ariana didn't have her fair share of hardships. "I spent many years not making much money. It's a challenge but it's also a great part of the creative challenge. I made those sacrifices for a life unstructured by industry."

Charissa Brock is a sculptor who works primarily with bamboo, often combining it with glass. Her studio is in Aloha, Oregon, just outside Portland.

Originally from New Mexico, she grew up in a house with an artist mother where making art was a natural part of being. By the age of eight she was already helping her mother in the glass studio, scraping kiln shelves and loading kilns. She grew up making all the time.

Charissa Brock

Wood

charissabrock.com

Photo credit: Noah Bell

"Bamboo Garden Nursery," work in progress.

"My parents gave us free rein with the power tools, the drills, the hammer, the screwdriver, the grinder, piles of different scraps of things...Rather than having Barbies while we grew up, we had Legos and scraps of wood and glass. I started developing skills early."

There was not a specific moment when Charissa discovered she was an artist; that part seemed to come naturally with her upbringing. It was during a college fair, when recruiters took a look at her portfolio and responded with positive feedback, that she first considered pursuing a degree and career as an artist. Charissa attended the Center for Creative Studies / College of Art and Design in Detroit, Michigan. There she took classes in several art mediums—metalworking, weaving, foundry work, sculpture—and earned a BFA. She later completed an MFA in fiber at Tyler School of Art.

When she was in her twenties, she headed to the Anderson Ranch to take a workshop with stick sculpture artist Patrick Dougherty. On the way, Charissa read an article in the airline magazine featuring the acclaimed contemporary basket maker Dorothy Gill Barnes. The article featured Gill Barnes in her late sixties working with a band saw. The image of a mature woman working with a substantial power tool sparked a desire within Charissa to learn how to work with tools so that she could manipulate harder materials. Reading this article was perfect timing for her, just as she was yearning to work with other, more substantial materials. She hadn't yet discovered working with bamboo.

Bamboo really drew her in. The first time she saw the material, it was love at first sight. She understood from the start that it would require a lot of work to manipulate bamboo, but for her, it

"Bamboo is a material that has a form when it is harvested from the ground. It requires deconstructing it to construct it, and there are so many possibilities in the material."

Tropical bamboo.

Studio.

"Mille Oculus" c. 2014, 34"×26"×6.25". Tiger bamboo, fused glass, waxed linen thread.

emanates an energy that has continued to confound her with its structure.

"With other materials that I laid my hands on, like clay or fabric, all of the inspiration seems to have to come from somewhere else; whereas with bamboo there is already inspiration in the materials because of the different ways it can be cut apart and be put back together…to create form out of it."

As a working artist, one of the challenges Charissa has had to maneuver is how little known bamboo is in the United States as compared to glass, which has a history and collector base in this country. For the most part, bamboo collectors in the United States look toward Asia, and more specifically to Japanese basketry. Yet in other ways bamboo offers an opportunity for her to present her work to a broader audience of collectors. "I have to walk a tightrope between several different areas. Between being a sculptor, which is what I consider myself to be, and being a craft artist or a fiber artist. That's a bit of a challenge but I also find it freeing because it means I can define where I show my work in several different ways."

"Spira Penna" c. 2014, 33"×13"×13". Tiger bamboo, fused glass, waxed linen.

Photo credit: Dan Kvitka

"From Land to Sea" c. 2014, 61"×6"×26". Tiger bamboo, stone, fused glass, waxed linen thread, paper, steel.

Charissa credits her friendship with Japanese bamboo artist Jiro Yanasawa with transforming her process of working with the material. When she moved to Portland, Jiro invited her to visit his studio and soon showed her how to properly split, shape, and build with bamboo. Prior to that she had improvised, which made the process much more difficult. Over a period of six to eight years, Yanasawa informally mentored her. She treasures the friendship they have maintained even though he relocated to his native Japan a number of years ago.

Over the years Charissa has built a multipronged business around her artistic practice. She refers to it as "spinning many plates at once." She offers three tiers of work and price points, shown at different types of galleries. There is a line of jewelry and a line of small-scale sculptures that are both shown in similar types of galleries in her local region, and she aims to expand their representation. The larger sculptures are created with the intention of showing them in major galleries and in two- and three-person traveling exhibitions. She teaches classes out of her studio, and occasionally travels to teach intensive workshops at craft schools and at the Oregon College of Art. She also works part time at the largest bamboo farm in the Northwest, which she absolutely loves.

"I'm able to be intimately involved with bamboo as a plant, and I understand how it grows and can learn about all the different varieties of bamboo there are in the world. I get to talk with

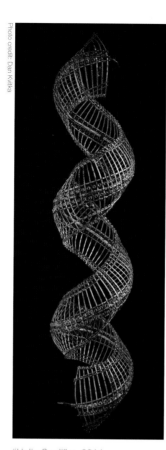

"Helix Oculi" c. 2014,
67"×17"×17". Tiger bamboo,
fused glass, waxed linen thread.

customers about bamboo. People know to find me there. It also provides a steady income…I don't have to have a factory project going on and can focus on the artistic aspect of my work."

Charissa's thousand-square-foot studio is detached from her house. It provides for the integration of life and work. The fact that she can eat in a much healthier way at home, that she can go to the studio before her son wakes up in the morning or after he goes to sleep, is a lifestyle choice that provides good rhythm and balance for her. "Having my studio at home makes me feel more like I'm always involved in the work rather than being separate from it. It helps my artistic process."

Along the way there have been a few sacrifices, the main one being a less active social life due to the time-consuming nature of her work. In the earlier part of her career Charissa was extremely driven and determined to get her work out into the world. It delayed certain aspects of her life, such as having children, until her late thirties. She explains, sounding especially sincere, that nothing has really felt like a true sacrifice to her because what she has feels rich to her.

Her aesthetic voice has become more focused as she matures as an artist. Early on her work's focus was more a play on materials, processes, and historical things to which she was attracted. Today Charissa finds her work to be more personal, reflecting relationships and narrative. She has learned to trust her response to a finished piece, looking for balance and beauty in the piece. She considers a piece to be successful when the outside world has the same reaction as she does. When she recognizes that there's some element that is slightly off balance in a piece, she has learned that it will take a little longer for the piece to find its owner. But it ultimately does.

"Lux Lucris" c. 2014, 22"×6.5"×40". Tiger bamboo, fused glass, cane, waxed linen thread, steel.

Jacob Brown

Metal

Jacob Brown grew up in a small town in the San Francisco Bay Area of California. He began his creative journey as a child, with parents who lived an art-filled life. In the 1970s, his parents and their friends would build large driftwood sculptures in the mudflats. Jacob says that he is a product of being raised in a community of craftsmen. "We were always making and creating. We had a giant roll of butcher paper that we would roll and out, and we'd draw forever. My backyard was a playground where we would dig giant holes and build sculptures." Jacob's neighbors when he was growing up, Michael and Ann Nourot, owned a glassblowing shop, and the neighborhood children would spend their weekends blowing glass and experimenting with small-scale sculpture.

Photo credit: Jacklyn Scott

"Trowel" c. 2012, 10"×3.5"×1". Forged steel, Wood.

When Jacob was twelve years old, he attended the California Blacksmithing Association Conference where Dave Nourot, a relative of the glassblowing neighbors, was a blacksmith at the event. It was at the conference that Jacob learned about the community, network, and utility that a life in the arts could give him.

Jacob would often go exploring in the Bay Area with his mother. One day, they were out running errands and stopped into an organization in Berkeley called The Crucible. A nonprofit fine arts organization, it was a community workspace that also held classes. "I walked into the waiting room and saw a bunch of really dirty, really happy metal workers giggling on the couch. They were probably laughing at me for being so lost but so intrigued. That's the moment I decided this was the life for me." Jacob volunteered for the studio on the weekends and after school, which afforded

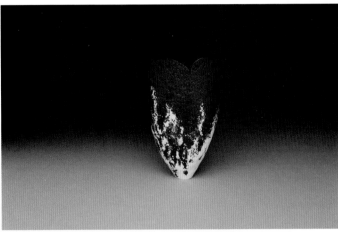

"Vessel #6" c. 2015, 9"×4"×12". Forged steel, paint.

"Vessel #7" c. 2015, 7"×4"×15". Forged steel, paint.

"Being an artist has meant living a simple life, but I've always chosen to live a simple life."

"The Fold" c. 2015, 4.5"×15". Forged steel, paint.

him free classes and a free education in welding and fabricating metal.

In high school, Jacob was accepted into an accelerated arts boarding school called The Oxbow School in Napa, California, where he concentrated in sculpture. The school had twelve students with six teachers, who broadened and fostered his imagination. Jacob earned his BFA in sculpture from the School of the Art Institute of Chicago and later traveled to Memphis, Tennessee, to work for the National Ornamental Metals Museum. He gained skills in historical repairs and large-scale commission ironwork.

After working at the museum Jacob traveled throughout the United States and Canada doing journeyman work, finally landing

Jacob at the forge c. 2015.

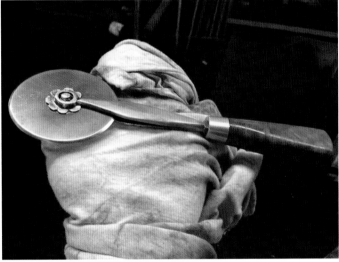

"Pizza Cutter" c. 2013, 10"×3"×1". Forged steel, curly maple, pewter.

at Peters Valley School of Craft to be an assistant in the blacksmith shop. "I originally came to work with Dick Sargent because I had heard he's a human encyclopedia for blacksmithing."

Historically the role of the blacksmith has been that of a community leader and an agent for change. Jacob works to promote the rejuvenation of the relationship between the art object and its maker, purpose, and audience. He feels that an artist's role is not only to create thought-provoking and beautiful objects, but also to serve the greater good in some way.

Jacob and fellow blacksmith, Sam Salvati, forge welding c. 2014.

Jacob generally starts his day with a scenic drive and a cup of coffee in the early hours of the morning. "Most of my life is pretty loud, so I like to sit and think when it's quietest and most people are still asleep." He uses this time to plan out a to-do list that contains shopping lists, daily goals, and long-term goals.

Watching Jacob work in the blacksmith shop is like watching a glassblower blowing glass, in that there is an elegant choreography between the peaceful heating of the metal and the mighty pounding of the power hammer. Based on the dimensions of the parent material and the tools available, Jacob makes decisions on the form and design of each of his vessels. However, due to the nature of the material, he must practice patience and often alter his plans to respond to the movement of the metal. "I always have an idea of what I want, but it usually evolves during creation. Sometimes I draw; sometimes I just play."

Sunshine Cobb began working in clay during her studies at California State University, and she graduated with her BFA in Studio Arts in 2006. She continued on to earn her MFA in ceramics from Utah State University in 2010. Sunshine is an entrepreneur known for her distinct bright matte-glazed functional wares. She relies on texture and color to create a sense of motion and time in her work. Her goal is to communicate how an object's significance can grow and change depending on the path of a person's life, and how the relationship between function and ornament shift throughout the course of a day, week, or a year.

Sunshine Cobb

Ceramics
sunshinecobb.com
instagram.com/shinygbird

Photo credit: Rachel Hicks

Sunshine glazing boxes.

"Installation Baskets" c. 2015, 10"×7"×5". Electric midrange red stoneware, coil built.

"There is a romantic fantasy associated with the word 'artist' that seems to negate the dedication, research, and passion that it requires to make the choices to be a successful artist. I also

"Traskets" c. 2015, 15"×6"×4". Electric midrange red stoneware, coil built.

"I try to engage a
nonmaker/nonartist
in a better
conversation, and
the possibility of a
meaningful
exchange."

"Installation Tea Tumbler Box Set" c. 2015, 7"×7"×7". Electric midrange red stoneware, coil and soft slab built.

refer to myself as a maker or designer and find that often conveys a better idea of what I do and how I see myself to folks who don't live this particular kind of life."

Sunshine, like many of the artists in this book, has used artist residencies at craft centers such as the Archie Bray and the Sonoma Community Center to help subsidize her practice until she developed the knowledge and resources to equip her own studio. In 2015, Sunshine opened her own maker space for creative minds called SideCAR Studio. As she builds her business, making pots is only one of the many things on her to-do list. Marketing, scheduling, traveling, and development of new business ideas have become huge parts of her "work," and managing those things is a constant balancing act.

"Bowls" c. 2015, 5"×5"×4". Electric midrange red stoneware, thrown.

While remaining humble about her 7,200+ Instagram followers, 500+ Twitter followers, and 3,000+ Facebook friends, Sunshine relies heavily on social media outreach to connect with her audience and direct them to her various sales platforms. Her income is generally divided fifty-fifty between teaching and sales of work via working with galleries, selling from booths at festivals, and sales through her website. Sunshine also spends several months traveling and teaching workshops around the country. "I have found that I excel in the areas of creative pursuits and that I have a passion for helping people find how to incorporate the handmade into their everyday lives. So I think I have adapted making a living out of needing to be a maker."

Kevin Crowe

Ceramics
kevincrowepottery.com

"I see my voice. It seems clear to me after all these years, but it is still out of reach; it is still developing…I feel overwhelmingly grateful for this life. Grateful that I get to do this; I'm a lucky guy."

The first time Kevin Crowe felt he had any artistic ability was as a young child. He was living in Japan and won an art contest; the prize was a class at a small art studio. In his later years, he gravitated more to the written word, and in college he loved music and poetry and majored in English, with aspirations of becoming a writer.

But at the age of twenty-three, an accident redirected his life. Kevin was hit by a truck while riding a motorcycle, and he broke many bones. Wrapped in bandages and casts, his mobility was extremely limited. His wife, who was just learning to make pots at the time, decided to take him along to the college studio where she was enrolled in a ceramics course. Kevin wasn't really all that interested, but since he couldn't do much else, he started reading the pottery books on the shelf. His healing process took many months. In reading Leach, Hamada, and Yanagi he found their philosophies about craftsmanship, humility, and beauty moving. He was already immersed in the writings of Gary Snyder, who to this day remains a great source of inspiration for him. It was a time when Kevin was figuring out how he was going to live his life with meaning.

One night, when no one else was in the studio, he decided to try throwing a pot on the potter's wheel. He was immediately taken by the sensation of throwing a pot. To him it was magical.

Photo credit: Tim Carlson, Studio C Photography

"Tea Bowl" 4.5"×4.5".

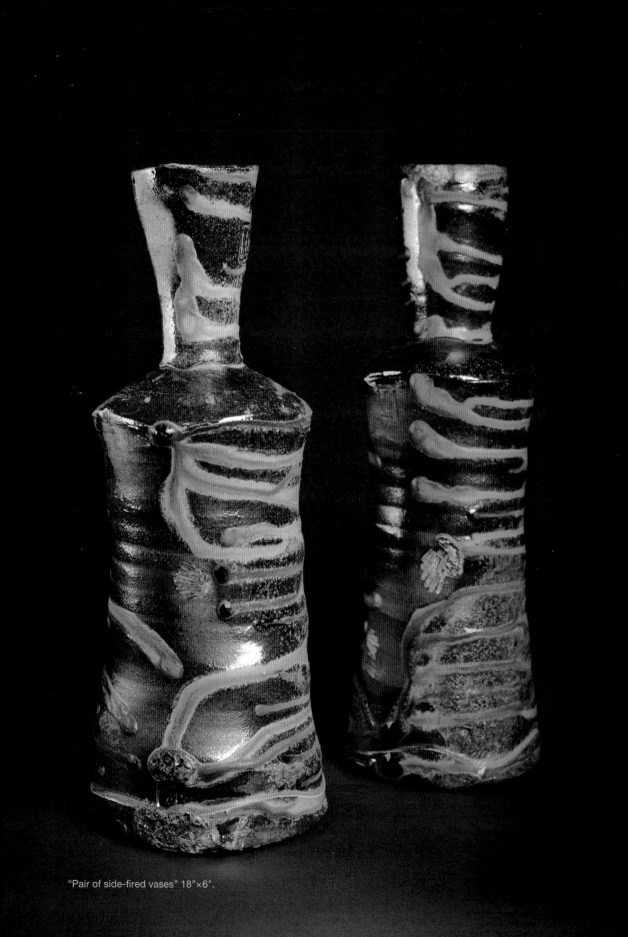

"Pair of side-fired vases" 18"×6".

Kai and Bram Crowe-Getty, Kevin's sons, assist in kiln building.

Kiln crew casting arch on new anagama.

It felt so good, so right, that becoming a potter seemed like a natural fit. For Kevin, clay work seemed to provide enough physical labor, together with a potential for intellectual stretching. "For some magical moments, I threw that first cylinder and all the apples lined up and I realized at about twenty-three that this was what I was going to do."

Teapot, vase, and lidded jar.

Determined to teach himself how to be a potter, he practiced throwing cylinders for six months, slicing them in half to check his progress. He complemented skill building with reading up on kiln designs, forming methods, and surface decoration, finally deciding upon wood fired pottery as the process and aesthetic that resonated with him the most.

"The other really strong simultaneous influence on my life was a poem that I read by Gary Snyder. At the time I could see parts of my life but couldn't articulate it as a whole or coherent position. Suddenly everything was clarified; I thought, oh, this is a life, a life I can pursue... The combination of community, of integrity of standards, of personal expression all very delicately rooted in tradition... that interesting brew of politics, of poetics, of Buddhism, of self-discipline was an interesting support system that allowed me to find some balance."

Another challenge along his journey was when the barn that he and his wife had been squatting in and making pots in was condemned to make way for property development. They quickly shifted gears and made the decision to purchase acreage in Virginia, with the notion that they could camp on site, build a studio and a wood kiln, and start production in maybe four to five

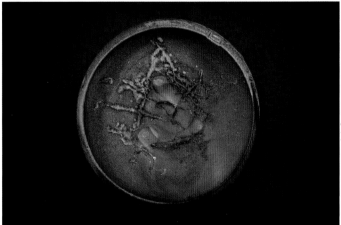

"Serving Platter" 3"×13".

months. It actually took them four years to first build their home and studio from reclaimed building materials and then to establish Tye River Pottery. For Kevin it was a profound experience to commit so much effort to a place and a task, with no really mature sense of how he would finance it or support himself. His decision was based on nothing more than that touchstone moment of throwing the first cylinder and deciding this was what his life would be.

"That moment of clarity (of throwing that first pot) supported me through confusion and frustration and improbability that I could build a house and studio. I used my skills as an English major, knowing how to research, and sort of cobbled it together. This taught me patience. It taught me what it was going to take if I was going to go deep into something. That if I really wanted to express myself I would need a whole lot more than just enthusiasm. It would take a lot of hard work, commitment, patience, and a sense of joy. Those four years were tricky. They were my primary source of education and shaped how I moved forward."

For more than forty years Kevin has been supporting himself and his family as a potter. For many years he also worked as a carpenter, ensuring that he made enough income to take care of his two sons. Kevin believes that diversifying is survival, and he maintains several income streams. He teaches a number of workshops at craft schools, at his studio, and at colleges on topics such as throwing large forms, kiln building, firing, and tea wares. His work is sold in galleries, during workshops, and at four studio sales annually. He also sells work through his website and online store. Over the years he has learned that income sources ebb and flow.

"When I was younger I always worried. I constantly worried about every kiln, every sale, worried about how it was going to work out. Sometime in my midforties I stopped worrying because I understood that if I keep showing up and keep committed…it will be okay. There will be lean times and better times, but it will be okay, so keep showing up."

"Clay…is such an elastic field. There is such a broad permission to explore, to express, that avoids the confinement that perhaps other traditions and other forms of expressions are hemmed in by. When I was younger I was an ideologue about function, but as time goes by I no longer see distinctions, and it has changed the way I pursue my work and my own expression."

"In [our] work as makers and as being part of a community of makers, the conversation should always get larger. Whenever I find myself in a context where either the ideology or particular aesthetic or technique or iteration begins to narrow and constrict, the only way to approach that situation is to enlarge it. Always allow for more questions. Always open up the edges. That sense of freedom and that sense of permission, I think Peter Voulkos has a big part in. It is something I try to emphasize when I am teaching…beware of diminishing functional work or the threat that sculptural work is an adversary."

Kevin took Gary Snyder's advice to his generation (a generation that was on the move) to heart. The message was to get to a place. Put down a root and make a difference. Be an artist in the community you live in and volunteer; don't yield to the temptation to cocoon in an artist's isolation. This ideology impacted the way Kevin set his roots within his community. He believes that community involvement begins to heal the perception of artists as being quirky and having a sense of entitlement and begins to replace it with the respect of the community and tradition.

Success, for Kevin, is not measured economically. In his world, success is linked to being married to a woman who is supportive of what he does, and who is patient with the controlled chaos of long wood firings. He says that it's important that this way of life is compatible with her goals. Choosing a life of an artist is one that is easy to do when you are single, Kevin points out, but once you have a partner and kids you are asking others to make sacrifices, too, so you have to find a balance in it.

"Finding a life that allows balance to those that you are sharing your life with, and keeping yourself economically stable, to me is success. That sounds as good as it gets. Also, walking out to the studio knowing I will always be slightly dissatisfied…"

There is a rhythm to the making that responds to the cycle of firing. Kevin's life experience and faith in living the life of a maker and his mindfulness have contributed to the success of his long career. Every afternoon he stops for tea with his apprentice. Having tea is a ritual pause in the day, during which they assess the accomplishments of the work flow when there is still one quarter of the day left to make adjustments.

"It's an opportunity to stop and breathe, because being self-employed has an urgency and a pace to it that, if you are not careful, can overwhelm you—and suddenly you seem to be chasing your life rather than living it."

Bruce Dehnert earned his degree in creative writing at the University of Montana and, while there, maintained a studio practice in the clay studio. After he graduated, Bruce's father asked him a very important question: "What are you going to do now?"

For the first time in his life, Bruce had found himself without a studio—and he realized that he wanted to be a potter. "That was the most important moment of my life, sitting in that car, at the base of the mountains, shooting the shit with my dad, and in that conversation, I made a commitment by saying it. By verbalizing something, there's a commitment made, at least in my mind. It's

Bruce Dehnert

Ceramics

brucedehnert.blogspot.com

"Ingot" 13"×12.5"×4". Woodfired.

"Nocturne Cherry" 13.5"×7.5"×12". Flashing slip, glazes, woodfired.

"GT2400's." Porcelain, flashing slip, glazes, woodfired.

"Tug" 13.5"×8.5"×9". Porcelain, flashing slip, glazes, woodfired.

not like a commitment to somebody else; it's a commitment you make to yourself." He had thought that being a writer, more specifically a poet or a playwright, is what he wanted to be, but he realized that the physicality and the community associated with being a maker was more important to him. He found himself drawn to the abstract self-expression that happens through the interaction with clay.

Bruce's college program required that he take at least one class a semester in another creative field, so he'd studied ceramics with Rudy Autio for three years. Rudy was a mentor to Bruce throughout his career, up until the day he died. Bruce loved the way Rudy worked because he broke away from the traditional brown pots and "really opened his eyes to the possibilities." Rudy

"A successful piece is going to be a piece that explains a time in which I live, in which there are these awful contradictions."

"Philostrophus" 41"×18"×24". Porcelain, glaze.

also provided support by offering advice and by recognizing skills in Bruce that helped guide his career.

Bruce has made a living by teaching workshops, writing, making functional and sculptural work, showing in galleries, and building kilns, and for the last thirteen years he has been the department head for ceramics at Peters Valley School of Craft in New Jersey. He tries to give a 100% commitment to each aspect of his endeavors, just as he would for any exhibition.

Kiln building is very intense and lucrative for Bruce, and it holds a special place in his heart, since he learned it from his dad. "It was a profound experience. I felt like I had a bond with my dad that none of my other siblings had. I even learned the birds and

"Ishmael Sent Away" 70"×39"×18". Earthenware, glaze, steel.

"Being able to capture the emotional connection to the mountains and to where I grew up was something I could do rapidly or take years to create, and that's the fluidity of the material that I love."

the bees from him on a kiln site. He knew no other way than to bring that up while we were building a kiln. It was so clumsy, but it is those experiences that have given me such a rich, broad, and interesting life."

Susan Peterson, ceramics program director at Hunter College, asked Bruce to move to New York City to teach for a semester at the college, substituting for a teacher who was out on maternity leave. He had never taught before, and boldly moved to the city, where his life changed dramatically. Having never made a study of art before, he made a point to go to every gallery and art museum possible in three months. Bruce discovered sculptural ceramics, something he hadn't really been exposed to in Wyoming, and decided to go back to school to get his MFA in sculpture. "Susan Peterson suggested I choose a school where I found a professor whose work I felt an affinity to, because they see the universe in the same way I do. Whatever their personality is, they tap into the same universal truths as I might." Bruce did his research and chose to go to Alfred University after learning about Tony Hepburn's installation work and Ann Currier's very clean and precise work.

Living the life of an artist has never been without compromises. Bruce gave up a financially stable life for a life rich with experiences and meaning. He says he was lucky to have parents who understood the difference between income and emotional or

"Gesthemane's Reflection" 39"×28"×19". Porcelain, glaze, steel.

cerebral success. They instilled values in their children that taught them that the money in their bank account did not equate to their value as a human being. "I had a paradigm shift, because I always thought I wanted to be a teacher. I'm thankful that I was a studio potter before being a teacher because I knew early on that I could always call myself an artist. There is a difference between teaching and working for an institution, and I realized that I didn't want to work for an institution." Bruce still teaches occasionally for a community college in New Jersey, but he spends most of his time teaching workshops for committed artists.

Every piece Bruce makes is like a poem, he explains; all of them are different, but they use the same language. When he starts a new body of work, he starts a new sketchbook. He treats each idea as something that he is going to explore for a long time. Once he determines what he wants to say, then "the possibilities are infinite."

"Red Room." Earthenware, porcelain, slips, glazes, various firings.

Bruce says the best thing he learned in grad school is to commit to a body of work and build on it in tiny increments by focusing on tactility and refinement. "I want to create some aspect, even a small one, like I might cut into a foot on things and leave a little tear. I am hyper-aware of that juxtaposition. I trim the feet on my pots, attempting to approximate industrial precision." He's been elected into the International Academy of Ceramics. Bruce is also pursuing his writing, having authored *Simon Leach's Pottery Handbook,* and he's currently writing a book on Takeshi Yasuda.

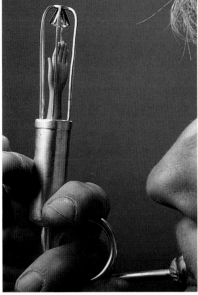

"Barbie Meets Sisyphus" 6"×1"×3".
Sterling, found object, CZ. Fabricated.

Sarah Doremus

Fine Metals
sarahdoremus.com

Sarah Doremus never thought she could be an artist. In fact, for many years she worked at Mount Auburn Cemetery in Cambridge, Massachusetts, handling integrated pest management. Having earned a degree in environmental communication at Antioch University New England, she later decided she needed a more creative career.

Sarah enrolled in an evening casting class at Massachusetts College of Art and Design and realized that metalsmithing was something that was realistically possible to do as a career. She went back to school to earn her BFA in sculpture at Mass Art. "I remember walking back from class and smelling the exhaust from the studio and thinking, 'I love that smell. I want to be an artist.'"

Sarah's interests in philosophy and in literature have given context to her artwork. Her kinetic jewelry is playful and witty while maintaining historical context and discussion of the human condition. Using found objects, doll parts, and metal, Sarah makes small-scale pieces that are intended to comment on body adornment and ornamentation. The work may even function in an absurd and completely unnecessary way. "I love asking questions when there are no answers. I thought about going to divinity school just to have that sort of meat to chew on for my art."

Sarah likes to experiment and play in the studio before finalizing a plan for a piece. "I measure once and cut twice." She often works on several pieces at once and will use parts from failed projects in a completely new piece of work.

Sarah supports herself through teaching elementary art, teaching summer workshops, and selling work through galleries. Her favorite gallery to sell work through is a vending machine. "A North Carolina–based artist, Clark Whittlington, started repurposing cigarette machines to sell art. It's called 'Art-o-mat.' A woman in Deer Isle bought one and I love selling work that way because

Photo credit: Rebecca Daugherty

"Take the Train" c. 2011, 2"×2"×1". Sterling, found objects, bearing. Fabricated.

"You always wish you were more successful. Teaching more, selling more, having more shows…I think it's characteristic of artists. J. Fred Woell, one of my mentors, once told me 'if you design your work to sell, you'll never succeed. Just do what speaks to you.'"

Photo credit: Maureen Farr

"Selfie Nation" 2.5"×.75"×.5". Sterling, copper, found objects. Fabricated, cast.

I make each piece in a sardine tin. I do a lot of plays on words. They sell for $10 apiece and I usually make 100 of them at a time." She finds that she loves this practice of creating egalitarian art that the rich, the poor, children, or adults can buy.

"Picketing Ring for the Lazy Protestor." Sterling, found objects. Fabricated.

"Fur-lined Wedding Rings" 1"×1"×.5". Sterling, copper, fur. Fabricated.

Photo credit: Maureen Farr

Sarah in the studio, 2015.

Most of her pieces are one of a kind, and therefore vastly different from one another. Sarah does not yet feel like she has found her aesthetic voice, but says that the fun part is the traveling you to do find it. "It's like a cone. I haven't tunneled to that point, but I'm not sure I want to."

Ellen Durkan grew up in Wilmington, Delaware, the oldest of nine children. She suspects that her parents kept hoping that they would produce an astrophysicist or engineer, but thus far their clan consists of artists and musicians. Ellen likes to believe that she started that trend.

From a very early age, draw̶̶̶̶ ̶̶̶̶̶med much of her time. Ellen was h̶̶̶̶ ̶̶̶̶̶l her the opportunity to take adult c̶̶̶̶ ̶̶̶̶̶unity center when she was fairly yo̶̶̶̶ ̶̶̶̶̶ she began college as a nursing ma̶̶̶̶ ̶̶̶̶̶t she needed to follow her passion in̶̶̶̶ ̶̶̶̶̶dergraduate programs at Delaware C̶̶̶̶ ̶̶̶̶̶Corcoran College of

Photo credit: Joe Hoddinott/Photography

Models Sabrina Carol and Jess McIntern, two of Ellen's "Iron Maidens." Leather, forged steel.

Art and Design, where she completed a BFA, and then attended Towson University where she received her MFA in sculpture in 2009.

At Corcoran she discovered a mentor, David Page, who worked in leather with a real focus on craftsmanship. The aspect of technical skill to execute work with precision drew her into working with craft materials and led her to metals. Skillful execution of craftsmanship is an aspect of her artistic practice that she finds more engaging than purely conceptual work, and is one reason why she designs and makes ornate iron corsets that are both wearable and sculptural. Ellen is grateful to have had a teacher like David Page who helped set her on a fulfilling path as an artist.

Ellen Durkan

Metal

ellendurkan.com
instagram.com/ellendurkan

Model at the DCCA Gala. Leather, forged steel.

While Ellen is in the early stages of her career, overcoming the debt of a valuable but expensive education requires her to have a resourceful approach to maintaining a steady income. Ellen teaches part time at Delaware College of Art and Design, bartends at night, operates her own blacksmithing forge in her growing metal shop, and is a certified yoga instructor. Her studio, business, and teaching life are very demanding of her time. By having her studio located at her parents' home, she can afford to spend more time there, rather than having to work to pay rent for studio space.

Ellen is determined to pursue her own business and eventually have a space where she will be able to accommodate working collaboratively with other artists. She applies for artist grants with a full understanding that some may be awarded and some may not be. (It was through a grant award that she was able to purchase the tools for her blacksmithing studio.)

Her corset series began from sculptural frames covered with fabric, which, to her, seemed unresolved. The moment of clarity came when she decided to create wearable sculptures entirely out of metal that she now combines with moveable parts and mixed media.

Her larger works are made on commission, typically through word of mouth connections, and her work has been featured at runway shows in both the United States and Australia. Ellen is passionate about building her collection of forged fashion attire to enable her Iron Maidens to strut down the runway.

Photo credit: Joe Hoddinott/Projexgraphy

"I'm an artist because I like a challenge. It's totally a challenge thing. When I want something to turn out a certain way and I work at it…I like to accidentally one-up myself."

Model Jess McIntern. Leather, forged steel.

Photo credit: Joe Hoddinott/Projexgraphy

Model Sabrina Carol. Leather, forged steel.

Her recently designed line of jewelry utilizes her creative and technical skills to earn a more steady income. Ellen believes that this production line work will be more accessible to the public, because "the market for metal corsets is limited."

Carol Eckert

Fibers

caroleckert.com

Carol Eckert recalls her college years, earning a bachelor of science degree in painting from Arizona State University, as her entrée into art. During college she began working in clay, which she really enjoyed, but the complexity of the process simply wasn't a good fit for her lifestyle.

As a way to solve her technical conundrum, she discovered she could make vessel forms out of clay, and vessels using basketry techniques. Carol's creative and technical leaps stem from the misinterpretation of a single picture of a Yoruba headdress. She imagined the ornate headdress, with its sculptural forms and beaded bird imagery, was constructed using basketry coiling techniques, when in fact the bird imagery was made with beadwork. Naïvely, she began to coil a simple little bird figure onto one of her vessels, then another, and from there Carol claims that

> "I spend a lot of time alone in the studio, and I love that part of it."

Carol in her studio.

her work exploded. She fell in love with the process, and to this day she enjoys the meditative process of building her work row by row.

By playing around with coiling basketry techniques she taught herself the fabrication method. Once she understood the

Drawing for "Time for the Ten Suns."

structural possibilities, coiling became the only technique employed in her sculptural basketry works, which have evolved in size from small hand held vessels to an installation measuring nine feet long.

"The way I arrived to coiling methods was through working in clay," Carol says. "It fits into my life, and it is so simple and free of technical requirements...I can just make the work and don't have to contend with a technical struggle. All I need is wire, thread, a needle, scissors, and sometimes a pair of needle nose pliers to make my work."

Carol's professional breakthrough occurred when she entered a small sculptural basket form into a competition at the Craft Alliance. The work was rejected. The rejection letter read, "Your basket doesn't fit the juror's concept." But soon after, out of the blue, she began to get opportunities to show her work. As it turns out, the opportunities came from Jane Sauer, who saw Carol's work at the Craft Alliance. Sauer is an artist, collector, and gallery owner who has been credited as being enormously influential, and at the time she helped expand and expose the fields of contemporary fiber and basketry. It was Jane who presented Carol's work to collectors. Prior to this turning point, Carol taught children's classes at her local art center part time. Once she started to show and sell work, she dedicated herself completely to her studio practice.

Having a studio at home works well for her because it provides the opportunity to pause and take little breaks, providing relief from the intensity of the detailed work. Carol plans out each piece

Working detail.

in drawings in advance, down to the colors. The drawings are then enlarged to scale, allowing for critical decisions to be made during the drawing stage before arriving at the construction stage.

To help with inspiration for future works, Carol began keeping journals with ideas as part of her practice. These physical journals have since been replaced with a Pintrest board.

"The work I admire is by unknown artists. I love art history and artifacts from the Egyptians, Mayans... Art history is where a lot of my inspiration comes from."

Liz Alpert Fay

Fibers

lizalpertfay.com

Liz Alpert Fay has always loved nature and credits her parents and grandparents, who fostered outdoor activities in her early childhood, with nurturing her appetite to observe patterns in nature and to use her hands skillfully. She attended the Philadelphia College of Art for three years and completed her studies at the Program for Artisanry at Boston University, earning a bachelor of arts in artisanry and textile design. She married a woodworker and both committed to a life as artist makers. They have raised two children who are now professional artists themselves.

After college Liz made art quilts for seventeen years and exhibited them nationally in venues like the American Craft Museum in New York (now the Museum of Art and Design) and in Japan. She was successful as an art quilt maker, and her work was collected and featured in major publications.

In 1998 she discovered the traditional craft of rug hooking and became immersed in the exploration of this very domestically

"Often, when working on pieces meant for the wall, I will experiment with unusual materials. Along with the fabrics, I might use paper, plastic, or other recycled materials. I have even hooked with grass and weeds!"

Photo credit: Brad Stanton

"Sycamore Trees: The Human Connection" c. 2012, 102"×102"×36". Wool, linen, batting, sycamore branches. Hand hooked, needle felted.

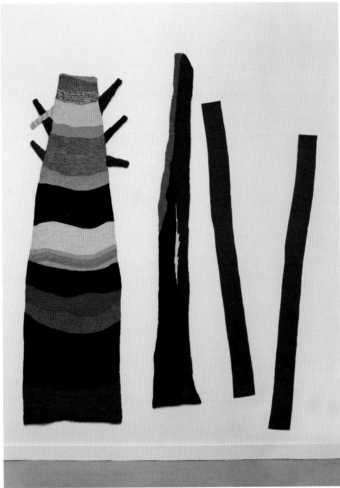

"The beauty and simplicity found in nature has always inspired me. An unexpected splash of color or the unusual twist of a branch has the ability to catch my eye and stay with me until these elements come together in my mind and become a visual language."

"Tall Trees" c. 2012, 89.5"×109". Wool on linen, hand hooked.

rooted American folk craft. She joined a group of "hookers" who would come together as a community to enjoy each other's company while hooking their rugs. In Liz's artful hands the materials began to evolve into contemporary themes. Her works were quietly narrative, even including translating her children's drawings into large-scale rugs, and she moved away from classic round shapes into a fresh realm beyond the tradition. Her use of color and inventive themes began getting her regional then national attention.

Ten years later, with enough knowledge of the field, she became the artistic director of the Newtown Hooked Art Shows. By creating an annual national call-for-entries exhibition she reached artists across the country who utilize rug hooking as their means of expression. Liz, along with her collaborators, succeeded in

Photo credit: Brad Stanton

"Blue Kylix" c. 2013, 12"×17"×13". Hydrangea petals, Japanese larch twigs, waxed linen.

Photo credit: Brad Stanton

"Bees in Trees Teapot" c. 2012, 11.75"×12.5"×12.5". Birch bark, reclaimed metal, waxed linen, Filbert branch, paper from wasp nest, dried plant material.

joining the community to present seminal exhibitions and expanded the field of contemporary rug hooking.

The interesting path this fiber artist has taken began with an unwavering commitment to her artistic voice. Liz has not compromised to sell work. She simply tightens her purse in pursuit of ideas. As a result of her work evolving conceptually, she has

"True North." Interactive piece. Showing progression.

moved away from making decorative work for high-end craft shows toward making work for exhibitions.

Liz is pensive, one could say introverted, an observer and thinker. She enjoys her contemplative tendencies because they inspire and lead her to following ideas until they can take form. No matter how long it takes.

Liz's studio is in her home. Early on she had to make space around her family. As her children went off to college and her work evolved, so has her need for space. Liz built a studio addition to her house.

Liz is particularly interested in challenging conventional ideas about what a rug is, and how it functions. By creating unusually shaped rugs, cutting and binding holes, and creating textures

Drawing design onto backing materials for a large hooked piece.

that beg to be touched, she strives to create a more interactive environment where the rug is no longer just a covering for the floor.

Since 2006 Liz has turned her attention to incorporating natural found objects that she collects during her nature walks into three-dimensional mixed media sculptures. Today, she is completely focused on exploring sculptural and conceptual installations using natural materials and fiber techniques. By getting involved in helping to further the field of contemporary rug hooking, she has crafted a community of rug hookers who are pushing the envelope thematically and technically. Although the way she works is very intimate and private, Liz maintains a robust website and communicates the evolution of her work via e-blasts and newsletters she sends every two months. Being engaging and consistent with her communications has helped her stay in touch with galleries, collectors, and friends.

Pat Flynn is an innovative goldsmith known for his elegant brace-lets and necklaces that combine blackened steel with 22k, 18k, platinum, diamonds, and pearls, and for his meticulous hinges and latches. He lives in High Falls, New York, where eighteen years ago he purchased a fixer-upper home that he took apart and modified to accommodate a studio. When he turned fifty years old he built a separate, larger, two-story studio building.

Pat's childhood was spent on a farm in Edinboro, Pennsylvania. The farm fostered his interest in working with his hands, figuring out how things work. He vividly remembers the first time he cut through a sheet of copper with a jeweler's saw (while in high school), because he instantly fell in love with the process. After briefly considering becoming a veterinarian, he decided to pursue an arts degree concentrating on jewelry and metalsmithing at Edinboro State College. A few years into his program of study, turmoil between faculty and administration disrupted the program,

Pat Flynn

Metals

patflynninc.com
instagram.com/patflynninc

Photo credit: Hap Sakwa

"Tapered Baguette Dust Cuff" c. 2013, 1.5"×2.25"×2.5". Fused 22k yellow gold on a formed iron cuff, with baguette diamonds set in 18k palladium white gold bezels.

so he applied and was accepted into the metals program at the State University of New York, New Paltz. By then he was in his late twenties, already married with a young son. As a student who had much more responsibility than his younger counterparts, Pat worked with a more serious focus and remembers being treated like a graduate student by the faculty. In order to support his family, Pat worked as a bench jeweler in a nearby shop and re-paired all sorts of jewelry while he completed a BFA degree in goldsmithing. The jewelry repair work was random, out of order, and taught him to develop a rhythm and discipline to complete

"Pebble Locking Bracelet" c. 2013, 1"×2.25"×2.5". Forged and fabricated iron locking bracelet with a box lock and hinge in 18k palladium white gold, and diamonds set in 18k palladium white gold bezels.

all the work at hand. The prolific hands-on experience he gained here helped him develop and hone his soldering and stone-setting skills. Perhaps the most important lesson, he says, was learning the joy of working at the bench—all the while being paid to do so.

"It's really important to practice your craft. I'm always trying to reach further to raise the bar." Prior to establishing his own business Pat worked in several capacities in factories as a shop foreman and manager. Working in the studio at night and on weekends, he quickly learned he was happiest working at his bench. It wasn't until the work started selling at the Greenwood Galleries in Seattle, Washington, and he was the recipient of two National Endowment for the Arts fellowships, that he finally believed that earning a living as a jeweler/metalsmith could be possible. Receiving the recognition was a validation of the direction his work was taking, and it really encouraged him to press onward.

His next step toward the success of his business was having his work picked up by Quadrum Gallery and Susan Cummins Gallery. Susan helped Pat develop exhibition catalogs and was the first to display his work at the Sculptural Objects Functional Art Expo in Chicago. The exposure and support he gained was a real career boost, despite a few challenges along the way.

Pat's secret to success is hard work and an adaptive business model. As a business owner with expensive materials and two employees, sustaining a consistent stream of income has required careful planning and risk assessment. Before a decision to

"Monolith Brooch" c. 2007, 3.75"×1.5"×.25".
Fused 22k yellow gold on iron with accents of
fabricated 18k yellow gold, and diamonds set in
18k palladium white gold bezels.

Pat Flynn forging c. 2013.

participate in an exhibit or event is made, Pat has to do a careful cost benefit analysis of participating in a retail show, the time away from working in the studio, leaving his crew to work on their own, travel costs, and potential sales.

Pat has carefully adapted the way his work enters the market as the economy and avenues to sell work have shifted over time. Ten years ago, high-end retail shows were a great source of direct sales for him, but in the current market that is not the case so only a few retail shows per year are on his calendar, primarily because Pat really enjoys connecting with the people who like to buy the jewelry.

His combination of selling through galleries and exhibiting at a select number of higher end retail shows seems to be working, and this has the added benefit of providing him with more time to work in his studio. Teaching is also a component that he's developed over the past few years, by offering two courses a year to up to four individuals on goldsmithing techniques. Pat really enjoys the individualized attention he can provide to students who come to him with an already advanced skill set.

"It's tough to keep it all going because the cost of materials is so exorbitant, preparing for a show can cause deficits, and if the show doesn't sell well, it is hard to bounce back. I don't live a luxurious life. I live a comfortable life. I have nice machines and a beautiful space to work in. I don't really want for anything, so I feel really lucky in that way."

Pat is fortunate to work with a handful of the galleries that first carried his work, and with a few newer galleries who also represent his work to a supportive clientele. Along the way to a successful career he says there have been "massive sacrifices; in a way, a couple of marriages (though not completely). I have denied myself tons and tons of stuff, going to the movies, reading a book, being warm; working when I'm injured. Most people don't want to work that hard and most don't want to make the sacrifices." All this because he is happiest when working in the studio

Bench room c. 2014.

making work that he hopes is authentic, that there is a market for, and that will bring people joy.

"I'm a jeweler-maker. It's the sort of world I revolve in. Making work and connecting with people who want to buy it."

When it comes to sources of inspiration, there are many artists and musicians who inspire Pat. Their influence is not so much the work but the feeling of the work: "how elements come together, that quality, that sort of feeling that piques your interest. It's those elements that I want reflected in my work. I am not interested in emulating other work."

Pat likes to work with wood as well as with metals. For him there's something about the accuracy of working with metal and the textural qualities that each of the metals he works with—steel, iron, and gold—provide that he finds intriguing. There is a particular aspect of the dichotomies of working with nonprecious and precious metals, of joining them together, that keeps him interested in the possibility facet of design.

For Pat, artist residencies and fellowships have been benchmarks in the development of his bodies of work. For instance, he says, being an artist in residence and the featured Master Metalsmith at the National Ornamental Metals Museum in Memphis were very enriching opportunities in his development as a master goldsmith.

Lindsay Ketterer Gates

Fibers and Metals

lindsayketterergates.com
instagram.com/lindsayketterergates

Lindsay Ketterer Gates is a mixed media artist who works from her home studio in Sparta, New Jersey. Her interest in art began very early on in her life, and as a child, she constantly fabricated projects from colorful paper scraps, tape, and scissors provided by her artist mother. She was perfectly happy having more art supplies than toys growing up. As the daughter of an artist who was always producing work and taking it to market, Lindsay grew up heavily influenced by a culture of making. During her teenage years, she had the opportunity to take weekend and summer courses at several prominent Philadelphia art schools, such as Moore College of Art and Tyler School of Art, and she ultimately chose to attend Kutztown University, where she received a BFA with a concentration in fibers.

Evident in her work is a love of fiber techniques, color pattern making, and connecting fibers, combined with a desire to create freestanding three-dimensional forms, which fiber resists with its soft nature. When Lindsay discovered wire looping she felt she had found the perfect material that can be manipulated like thread and is strong enough to provide the structure needed for freestanding forms. Lindsay's work has evolved into intricate compositions created with the inventive use of common materials. Using slightly obsessive methods and quantities of materials she combines mixed media work and a love of fiber techniques with

"Calendula" c. 2015, 29"×13"×6".
Stainless mesh, paint, coated copper wire, steel, patina.

a curiosity for all things purchased in bulk. Random industrial materials are combined with tedious hand-manipulated wire looping to mimic or simply give a nod to beloved textile accents, patterns, and details. The vessels, although fabricated using hard, industrial washers, joiner biscuits, cotter pins, and more, start to read as soft decorative elements.

Lindsay reflects on the conscious decision to work with processes that require little infrastructure, freeing her to make anywhere, and utilizing materials that are relatively inexpensive.

"Lily of the Valley" c. 2015, 29"×18"×6".
Stainless mesh, paint, coated copper
wire, steel, patina.

"After college, I had to consider that I could stop making things and use the excuse of not having the space or not having the money to purchase materials. Or, I could change what I was making and keep making."

"Silver Peacock" c. 2015, 19"×11.5"×6". Stainless mesh, paint, coated copper wire, aluminum ring.

Requiring only a small studio space and employing common materials has allowed her to move and continue making no matter what.

During college she completed a summer assistantship residency at Peters Valley School of Craft, where she discovered the possibility of a whole new way of life, doing what she wanted to do. She was fortunate to have met John Garrett, a contemporary basket artist, while managing the fibers studio after graduation. Garrett invited Lindsay to show her work as an emerging artist at the Society of Arts and Crafts in Boston. This exhibition was a turning point for her budding career because it put her work in front of collectors, gallery owners, and on the cover of *Metalsmith* magazine.

Early on she sold work at major craft shows such as the Philadelphia Museum of Art Craft Show, the Smithsonian, and Craft Boston. Showing at these venues helped build her collector base and relationships with gallerists such as Duane Reed, Jane Sauer, and Bruce Hoffman, to name a few. She feels gratitude and loyalty to the galleries who have taken a risk with her work and have provided her with opportunities to show work that is now in prominent museum and private collections.

"I work like a dressmaker with paper patterns... Every step is sequential."

"Celestial Navigation" c. 2014, 24"×12"×6. Stainless mesh, paint, coated copper wire, steel, patina.

"Kylix in Blue" c. 2014, 19"×11.5"×6". Stainless mesh, paint, coated copper wire.

"I never waver from that gut feeling, never push through a piece if I get that feeling that the piece is not working. I just don't go any further, no matter how far along I am in the process. I think that's really critical."

Lindsay earned a graduate certificate in arts administration from Seton Hall University and worked for several arts councils before becoming the Development Director at Peters Valley, where she enjoys being part of a creative community of makers. Having a job provides her the freedom to make whatever she wants and allows her to spend exorbitant amounts of time developing the detailed intricacies of her work without consideration of the cost of production. Lindsay is driven by a total commitment to excellence. "The end result is what matters. How much time it took you does not."

"Year of the Snake" c. 2014, 16"×15"×7". Stainless mesh, paint, coated copper wire.

"Double Loop Teapot" c. 2015, 11"×10"×5". Pistachio shells, beads, coated copper wire, paint, stainless mesh.

People started calling Glenn Gilmore an artist before he was ready to give himself that title. He never studied art specifically, instead taking classes in machine shop and welding. After mastering those basic skills, he had an interest in decorative metals and enrolled in a few jewelry classes at a local community college. Glenn's parents were both educators and had an inquisitive way of looking at the world, particularly in terms of geology and architecture. They often took Glenn to the art museum; these excursions formed the basis for his exploration of art later on.

Glenn attended the Wolverine Farrier School in Michigan in 1974. After honing his forging abilities, he moved into horseshoeing competitions that helped improve and focus his skills. A friend introduced him to *Edge of the Anvil* by Jack Andrews, which inspired him to learn more about the decorative side of metalworking. In 1978 Glenn attended a conference held by the Artist-Blacksmith's Association of North America (ABANA) in Purchase, New York. This solidified his departure from horseshoeing and led him into studying with Francis Whitaker at the John C. Campbell Folk School. Glenn soon received a creative artist's grant to study pattern-welded steel. He spent two weeks working with Daryl Meyer, producing a series of forged pieces with an accompanying booklet detailing his findings.

In 1983, he moved to Tennessee to work as a blacksmith at Silver Dollar City. However, when he arrived, he was told that the blacksmith position was no longer available but that they really needed a glassblower. "I convinced them I could be their

Glenn Gilmore

Metals

gilmoremetal.com
instagram.com/glenn_gilmore

Photo credit: Tommy McNabb

"Decorative Railing Panels" c. 2003, 28"×96"×4". Forged steel.

> "I often take photos of nature to bring [those] elements into my designs. I make sure my designs are cleaner and more graceful curvilinear views. I can't always do it, but I strive for it. Most people won't look that closely, but for the one person who will, that craftsmanship will be there."

"Detail of Decorative Railing Panels" c. 2003, 18"×36"×4". Forged steel.

glassblower, and I was for two years. There are crossovers between forged metal and blowing glass so it was an easy transition." After attending the ABANA conference in 1984, Glenn decided to go to Germany for four months to study with Manfred Bredohl, who was running a program for Americans to learn about European styles of ironwork. "Studying in Germany had its own set of challenges, but being immersed in the history of the European ironwork was an amazing opportunity. I realized one thing, though. They have all the same problems we do!" Bredohl gave his students an all-encompassing experience, teaching them about both design and the business. Moving back to the States marked a major shift for Glenn. He started working bigger and with more decorative elements. He spent the next two years as a resident blacksmith at the John C. Campbell Folk School, and amassed a body of work to present at the American Craft Council Winter Market in Baltimore. After a few years of making and selling wholesale work, commission work took over his business.

Glenn has been fortunate enough to have a steady client base that has consistently given him work. "At this point, I would like another smaller product line for a supplemental income. Commission work is great, but it's one giant deposit that thins out before the next project starts. It would be nice to have a steady cash flow as well." Glenn can sustain his commission work because he is very particular about his craftsmanship. "I have some clients that don't even ask the price anymore. It's great knowing that someone can have that level of confidence in you because they know that whatever it is, it's worth it."

Photo credit: Tommy McNabb

"Prairie Star Chandelier" c. 1994, 18"×36"×22". Forged and fabricated steel.

"Twig Railing" c. 2006, 36"×240"×4". Forged steel.

Glenn knows that his work will be around for a very long time for people to enjoy. He loves interacting with clients. For Glenn, success is not defined by how much money is in the bank, but by knowing that he successfully supported his family, running his own business since 1985 and making it through the ups and

"Foliage Gate" c. 2015, 52"×96"×4". Forged steel with polychrome powder coat finish.

Glenn forging railing cap c. 2015, 138"×2.5"×.75". Forged steel.

downs of the changing economy. He has learned to deal with difficult design conflicts and installation issues. "Pay attention to your math teachers and your English teachers. You need math to figure stuff out and you need to know your English to communicate with your clients." He now runs his own shop with a crew,

"Crab Grill" c. 1998, 48"×32"×4". Forged Monel 400, mortise and tenon joinery.

often working long hours to complete jobs. There are many obstacles in the field, but Glenn knows that taking the time to make sure each step is done as well and as accurate as possible saves him time later on.

Martha Grover

Ceramics

marthagrover.com
instagram.com/marthahgrover

Martha Grover's pottery is a beautiful example of the delicate feminine forms that can be created with porcelain clay. She learned to throw in high school, but never saw it as a viable career option. Coming from a family of engineers, it made sense for her to pursue something within a more technical school of thought. Martha majored in architecture at Bennington College. During an internship, she worked in a few architecture firms and realized, "I would spend the first ten years of my career on a computer drafting someone else's work. I'd probably go out of my mind!" She began to take classes in the college's clay program and realized that she might actually be able to make a living doing what she loved: making pots.

"Clay is such a malleable material. It can really become anything…The sky is the limit. You can make it look like cardboard, wood, or even a rock. I try to make it look like fabric and flowers." Martha says it's the unlimited span of possibilities and the tradition of utility that draws her to clay. Her goal is to make pieces

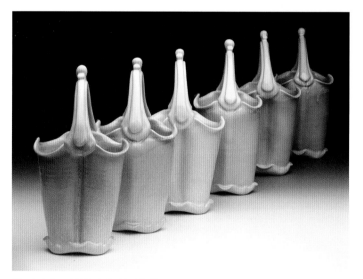

"Baskets" c. 2015, 11"×6"×5". Thrown and altered porcelain.

with a connection to the human world, be it a mug or a plate; each object plays a role in everyday life. Her work with porcelain particularly has a seductive translucency that gives it an otherworldly quality. She derives inspiration from the world around her. "There is a little orchid show I always make sure I attend because I really integrate those lines in my work. I draw a lot from the world around me. My husband is a photographer, and he often makes me stop so he can take photos of a crack in the sidewalk for twenty minutes to an hour. It makes me look at the details of the

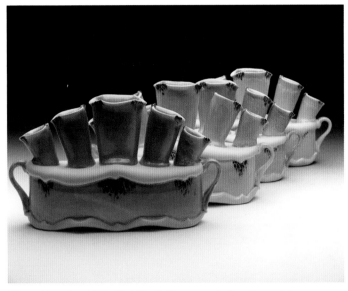

"Fluted Vases" c. 2015, 7"×12"×4". Thrown and altered porcelain.

world in a way I probably would have passed by. My creative time is when I'm out in the world."

Much of Martha's work is sold through retail galleries and shops on consignment, as well as through her Etsy store online. She has a selection of shapes and colors that she often employs in her work, but she enjoys a challenge and is often invited to exhibitions that require her to explore new areas and forms. "I started making lidded forms for a show about butter and some mojito juicing pitchers from an alcoholic beverage show. When I have a new form to make, I might sketch five ideas in clay before I decide that it's the path to take."

Martha earned her MFA from the University of Massachusetts Dartmouth, studying with Rebecca Hutchinson and Jim Lawton. Early on in her career, Jim nominated her as an emerging artist at the National Ceramics Conference, resulting in national exposure, and she was soon featured on the cover of *Ceramics Monthly*. She then became a resident at the Archie Bray Foundation for the Ceramic Arts in Helena, Montana. "My residency at the Bray really opened doors for me that might not have happened otherwise. Surrounding myself with like-minded peers and watching them make work, build studios, and make ends meet was the best education for me. Everyone has something different to teach and share."

Martha loves the community that comes along with clay. She realizes that there is more success to be gained as a team than

"My heart is more full when I'm making pots."

Martha throwing c. 2015.

by each person individually and plans to organize an artist guild in her area of Maine. Her studio is cozy, rural, and secluded. "It's really small and most of our belongings are in storage, but we are used to tight living spaces...We live simply, not spending money on frivolous things. We miss out of some of the social aspects, but we're really dedicated to our work and living simply has allowed us more time in the studio and to be able to travel."

Studio c. 2015.

She teaches between six and eight workshops around the United States annually. Otherwise, she is in the studio making pots, estimating about 150 pots per month. She doesn't generally think about the income that these pots yield, but rather about her growth as an artist. "As long as I feel like I'm making good choices in what I'm making, how it visually and functionally works, then I feel successful. It's more than what is at the bottom line at the end of the month. So far, my decisions as an artist have coincided with making money."

"Nesting Bowls" c. 2015,
7"×7"×4". Thrown and
altered porcelain.

Pitcher rims (detail) c. 2015,
9"×8"×6". Thrown and altered
porcelain.

CJ Harker

Photography

cghphotography.net
instagram.com/damagednotions

As kid, CJ Harker rode around his hometown of Trenton, New Jersey, on a skateboard with a disposable camera. A friend of his attended the University of the Arts in Philadelphia, and CJ would often help him with his photography assignments, thus gaining a good deal of technical experience. It sparked a fire in him to delve deeper into the practice, and he quickly purchased more photography equipment.

However, he considered photography as merely a hobby. "I was programmed to think that graduating high school and going to college for a business degree was the normal thing to do." So CJ did just that; he went to college for three semesters, studying social economics and political science. Dissatisfied, he quit school and worked for a few years as an auto body mechanic, installing audio equipment. While working full time, CJ decided to enroll in photography classes at the community college down the street to keep him in the darkroom and involved in the photography community. He soon reached his limit of classes at the community college and decided to apply to the University of the Arts in photography, where he explored the possibilities of the medium.

During this time, he became involved in the skating scene in Philadelphia, and would spend hours shooting photos of the skateboarders. He became a regular contributor to his friend Marcus Waldron's zine, *Skate Jawn*, where he still publishes many of his photos. CJ feels the zine is a place where the two worlds of photography and skateboarding merge beautifully. "*Skate Jawn* is a labor of love. It is a publication that is distributed through

"Meg C" c. 2013, 5"×7". Wet collodion tintype.

"I like new things that push the boundaries, both in art and music. I want to push my boundaries and the boundaries of my medium."

"If you do what feels right to you and follow the path that you want to be on, doing it with the right intentions and living positively, then things have a way of keeping everything moving forward."

"Will K" c. 2013, 8"×10". Wet collodion tintype.

local skate shops. It will probably never be something that I'll get a paycheck from, but it's something I'll probably never stop doing." With the growth of digital photography in the last decade, this zine is a way for CJ to put something tangible in the world that adds culture to photography.

CJ spent a summer as a photography assistant at Peters Valley School of Craft in Layton, New Jersey. There, he met photographer Craig Barber, who introduced him to wet-plate collodion work. "I still use that process as often as I can. Craig was someone I clicked with so well with; we were on the same page about almost everything. He has so much more experience than I do and he was able to broaden my outlook and perspective on so many different things." CJ attributes much of his inspiration and knowledge to the instructors, like Craig, that he met that summer.

He claims that the best thing photographers and makers can do for themselves and their careers is to always surround

CJ at work c. 2015.

themselves with like-minded people who are on similar creative paths. Whether it be assisting in workshops, volunteering to help local photographers, or assisting in classes at colleges, he continues to maintain a presence in the photography community. "There is still so much to learn. Everyone has something different to offer, and working with different people can give you practical information as well as technical information and they can help you make connections in the industry."

CJ feels it is important to remember that everyone will have compromises and choices to make in life in order to succeed. He learned early that success doesn't happen overnight and that you will eventually take more steps forward than backward. He admittedly does not self-promote heavily on social media. He says that his formal gallery photography should remain just that, and therefore uses social media to broadcast visuals into his daily life.

His recent body of work is focused on a local blacksmith shop in Trenton that caught his attention while skating. "One day I stopped in. It was like a light bulb turned on." He likes this space of a male dominated realm because he feels that it is easily accessible. As a photographer, he finds it important to be nonintrusive

Issues of *Skate Jawn* and publication work CJ has done for University of the Arts.

or distracting to capture an authentic view, and he easily blends into environments like a skate spot or a blacksmith shop.

Looking ahead, CJ isn't ready to commit to one particular style of working and is exploring different avenues by participating in various artist residencies. "I have my vision and technique. I don't want to get stuck in a rut."

Andrew Hayes is careful not to label himself an artist, but rather, refers to himself as a sculptor. His work is primarily made of altered books and steel, speaking to knowledge of strength and industry. Andrew attended Northern Arizona University in 2004, but found that the sink-or-swim mentality of the traditional college format didn't work for him. He worked in a factory as an industrial welder and would quit periodically to work in the studio to make art.

He received a five-year Core Fellowship at Penland School of Crafts, where he gained a huge education from the community of artists and visiting artist workshops throughout the year. He later apprenticed for metal sculptor Hoss Haley for three years, where he gained much of his education. Today, Hoss acts as a great support for Andrew, helping him navigate and build his own career.

While Andrew is still early on in his career, being a resident artist has allowed him time to incubate his ideas and explore other mediums to incorporate into his steel sculptures. He does commission work, when necessary, which allows him to have income to support his creative practice. "It seems like a total luxury to have art and to live with art, but I tell myself that there is something important about being surrounded by so much of it. We are exposed to so many visually intriguing things through social media, and I feel a little silly thinking that I should be able

Andrew Hayes

Metal / Mixed Media

andrew-hayes.squarespace.com
instagram.com/andrew_hayes_studio

Photo credit: Mercedes Jelinek

"Station" c. 2015, 18"×18"×8". Steel and book paper.

Andrew in front of his studio.

to do that for people; it feels wrong that I should have the audacity to think that I could give people that feeling. But there is something about just wanting to make these shapes, and wanting to work with these materials, and wanting to understand how things go together in a pleasing way."

Andrew employs used books to form lines and movement set within hard steel framework. The content of the book does not matter so much to him, but the shades of black that occur from the remnants of text can build their own story for the piece. Utilizing paper in his body of work allows for greater abstraction and an exploration of curvilinear forms.

"Sometimes someone comes in and they want a stand or they want something that isn't necessarily my artistic vision, but in making it, I'm learning a lot. At the same time, it's taking me away from the work that I want to be making, but it's helping me survive

"Dure" c. 2015, 12"×7"×6". Steel, book pages, paint.

"Pip" c. 2015, 7"×5"×4". Steel and book pages.

"Grasp" c. 2015, 15"×5"×2". Steel, book pages, bronze.

Andrew cutting metal.

and I'm making money and I'm still working with my hands. I'm still learning how to do something that I might not have done otherwise. It gets me to kind of get my head up out of the sand and see how to confront a new challenge."

Having grown up on a farm in Idaho, Jan Hopkins spent most of her childhood playing with sticks and mud, creating a fantasy world of her own. As a young adult she worked in property management and also ran the administration side of her husband's illustration business.

The artist within her didn't begin to emerge until she was already a mother and her family relocated to Washington State in 1988. She was introduced to Native American basketry at the Heard Museum and began taking courses at the Basketry School in Seattle. Her fascination with basketry and materials gathered from nature quickly became a self-proclaimed obsession. After learning processing techniques from Northwest Coast native basket makers and contemporary instructors who taught a foundation

Jan Hopkins

Fibers

janhopkinsart.blogspot.com
instagram.com/janhopkinsart

Photo credit: Mari Hopkins

Jan and Chris looking over current immigration/internment project.

Son Justin Hopkins, also an artist, is working on Jan's family immigration/internment project.

of traditional and technical skills, she realized how much the basketry tradition relies on natural materials whose harvesting is being restricted to guard against depletion.

Jan asked herself, "Why aren't we experimenting with the things in our environment? There is such an abundance of material… Everyone has an orange…" She felt the need to select her own readily available materials, and by working with them began to develop a unique "voice" of her own. The only traditional material she uses is yellow cedar bark, and she has successfully developed ways to use citrus peels, cantaloupe peels, pomegranate peels, sturgeon skin, petals, leaves, seed pods, and other natural materials into her work.

"Contemplation" c. 2004, 72"×14"×12". Organic fiber sculpture, agave leaves, yellow cedar bark, waxed linen. Hand sewn together with variations of looping technique.

Jan continues to make basketry and container-like objects such as teapots and shoes. The year 2000 was a pivotal year—she moved forward and started to create more challenging forms, such as her first female torso. In constant search of a challenge, in 2006 Jan added a visual narrative that included familiar quotes by people that she admires, designing around the persona of those who inspire her. "My series, 'Women Icons,' is not about flawless, perfect, super-human women, but women who faced strong adversity and despite this, lived iconic lives."

"Oh Eleanor" c. 2012, 30.5"×28"×12". Cantaloupe peel, ginkgo leaves, ostrich shell beads, cedar bark, waxed linen.

After her first feature in a national exhibition, Jan was introduced to influential gallery owners Jane Sauer and the Coopers from Mobilia Gallery. Mobilia Gallery took Jan's work to SOFA Chicago in 1999. (Jan remembers being so impressed to see her work displayed next to Ed Rosenbach's.) Her career took off when the Jane Sauer Gallery began selling everything Jan could produce. This fortunate exposure and connection to Jane Sauer demanded her total and complete commitment to making the work. Jan had to stop working for her husband's business, and had to stop showing with other galleries, to focus entirely on her studio practice. Often working seven days a week for up to fourteen hours

"I don't need to draw what I envision…If I draw an idea, it feels like it is set in stone."

"Oh Eleanor (detail)" c. 2012, 30.5"×28"×12". Cantaloupe peel, ginkgo leaves, ostrich shell beads, cedar bark, waxed linen.

a day, she had to find ways to juggle her production and family life.

"I think my whole career has been lucky, unexpected and not planned…like I just fell into it…like it's too much. In fact, it felt overwhelming at times."

Jan also credits her galleries for encouraging her to focus on the quality and the excellence of her work, without worrying about the cost. She has certainly followed their advice. Her work has gotten larger and more narrative as her ideas evolve. Her home studio began as a small space that now has spread into her husband's studio area (he built a separate outbuilding a number

"Girl Power (Wonder Woman Shoes)" c. 2011, 7"×4"×9". Lunaria seed pods, grapefruit peel, canary honeydew, cantaloupe peel, yellow cedar bark, waxed linen. Hand-sewn paper/plaster molded shoes.

of years ago), and this has allowed her to continue to experiment freely. Perhaps the biggest sacrifice Jan has made for her career is her lack of time to participate in extended family gatherings such as weddings or family vacations with her husband and children. Yet Jan and her husband, Chris, found ways to carve out family time during some of his professional illustration engagements that required travel. By bringing the family along, they combined work with quality time together.

Jan's process is based on curiosity and experimentation with many aspects of fabrication based on techniques she has developed along with traditional ones. When asked if she keeps a journal of ideas, Jan admits to having dealt with a reading disability as a child. She learned better by listening, and has since developed the ability to visualize in great detail the work she wants to make. It is hard to imagine the complexity of her work not emerging from sketches, but it doesn't.

Her narrative work has become more articulated, and she now focuses on themes. Her upcoming body of work is deeply personal and routed in her Japanese American heritage. "This is proving to be another pivotal year, as my obsession has evolved around creating a visual art journal involving my cultural identity. I grew up not knowing about my Japanese heritage. In fact, I didn't realize I was Japanese until I was in the fourth grade. I later found out that my brothers, sisters, and friends had the same experience. As I research, I am finding a treasure trove of history in my family's background that was rarely if at all spoken of...[including] during World War II the relocation of my parents' entire family from Seattle to Minidoka relocation camp in Idaho."

"My husband Chris, our son Justin [both fine artists], and I are embarking on a new project, creating work we plan to exhibit in the future. We will create paintings and sculptural work depicting my family history, including the incarceration and the emotional, social, and economic effect it had on three generations."

"It is important to know your heritage, and I feel an urgent need to begin this project in part for my father [100 years old] and my uncle [101 years old], who are the last that remain of the previous generation and who were interned during World War II. I am also compelled to work on this for those who have experienced the same background as my parents and grandparents and me. I want to honor the generations that gave me a better life."

Jan stays connected with her collectors and friends through an active blog and Facebook artist page. Her most recent obsession is Instagram, which she describes as "opening up a book of beauty."

"My work is built on a solid foundation, but slowly changes and evolves."

Michael Hurwitz

Wood

michaelhurwitzfurniture.com

Michael Hurwitz is a furniture designer based out of Philadelphia. He earned his BFA from Boston University in 1979, studying under Jere Osgood. Michael recalls an assignment Osgood gave him, which was to build a chair 7 percent above the breaking point. The assignment was open to interpretation, but the idea was to think about structure as design, and not to overbuild. That one assignment, Michael says, became a lifelong directive for his work. "Sometimes, I make a chair or a table, but it's the same idea. I allow the structure to determine the design."

Photo credit: Dean Powell

"Chinese Piece with Cracked Ice" c. 2006, 68"×36"×20". Zelkova, bamboo, Damascus steel, bronze pulls.

"Wormy Wall Vase" c. 1994, 42"×11"×51.5". Silver leaf over wood, bronze vase etched through with copper tube and liner.

Michael went to college originally intending to study instrument making, but he fell in love with furniture making. Wood has a resistance of material that he enjoys, along with having a history in furniture, in the building of ships, and—most interesting to him—in the building of machinery during the Victorian era. He is careful in his work not to add elements that are merely ornamental; rather he integrates them to create a cohesive whole.

Michael hopes to never have a trademark style like those that made Nakashima and Maloof household names. For him, "style" has more to do with a point of view, or a way of arriving at a form, than it does with having a consistent visual language. Regardless,

"To be successful is to be allowed or able to continue."

"Collector's Cabinet" c. 2003, 60"×34"×20". Zelkova, silk with epoxy, copper pulls.

he believes that the viewer who is familiar with the field, and who looks carefully, should still be able to recognize his work.

After his graduation, Michael joined a cooperative woodshop with fifteen to twenty woodworkers. This space allowed him to work on lucrative jobs such as making kitchen cabinetry, while still affording him time to make speculative furniture. When money was tight, he would work for the fellow woodworkers in the co-op.

"Twelve Leaf Resin Table" c. 2012, 16"×40". Ash, wenge, epoxy resin.

Michael's studio assistants c. June 2015. From left to right: Atsuko Hanano, Zack Deluca, Emily Bunker.

Michael went on to teach full time in Philadelphia for a period of five years, which enabled him to purchase a building that acted as a studio and a home, and also as rental space for additional income. In addition, the Peter Joseph Gallery began to represent Michael, giving him a stipend, which he then used to hire an assistant. Every two years, the represented artists would have a solo exhibition, resulting in commission work.

When the economy collapsed in 2008, Michael sold a piece of property he owned in Philadelphia, and that afforded him time to relocate his studios and rent out the old space. He often reminds himself that despite at times having to work for an extremely low hourly wage, he is constantly building a portfolio of images that

Studio photograph with chair mock-up c. June 2015.

can later be used to apply for grants, fellowships, or residencies. "Residencies are a great way to develop as an artist and make work in a sort of 'semi-protected' environment—an environment where lack of money is less of an issue."

Being an artist isn't always easy. In fact, Michael finds that he often makes compromises to afford himself time in his studio, like being the maintenance man for his rental units. These tasks help him avoid making compromises in the studio. He finds this lifestyle to be very rewarding. Michael's daughter is planning to attend art school; he's told her that she is going to spend most of her life working, so she'd better love it.

Beth Ireland is a conceptual sculptor. Drawing upon a lifetime of traditional woodworking skills, she explores sculpture, architecture, and relational aesthetics. Her belief in the power of the object drives her work, exploring the idea of memory locked in

Beth Ireland

Wood

bethireland.net

objects and the creation of object as a visible symbol of memory. Working alone and collaboratively, she delves into the anthropological meaning of making in our modern lives.

Beth's career has been filled with interesting turns, driven by her curiosity and sense of adventure. When she was a child she told her father that she wanted to be carpenter and a psychiatrist, and now chuckles about how it all turned out. During a summer college break she found herself in need of a job. She started designing, making, and selling leather bags, and was able to earn a living. This venture made her aware that she could support herself by making things and gave her to confidence to join a carpentry crew upon completing an undergraduate degree in art education and illustration.

"Four Eyes" c. 2013, 7"×57". Holly, mahogany.

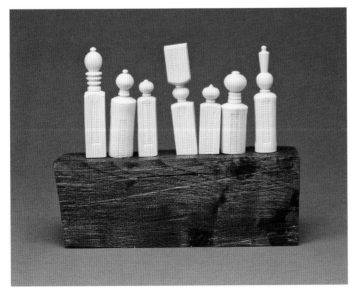

"Totem 1" c. 2011, 9"×6". Cherry, holly.

"Pencil Box" c. 2013, 44"×15"×12". Bass wood.

"To-Go" c. 2014, 46"×24". Bass wood, milk paint.

"Hee-Haw" c. 2011, 5"×8". Ambrosia maple.

"Self-portrait" c. 2010. Installation. Mixed media.

"Instruments" c. 2015, variety of sizes. Mixed media.

"Being a woman has been a challenge in the career that I chose because for the last thirty years I worked for contractors and builders. Consider that in high school they wouldn't allow a girl to take drafting class. Then in the early 1980s men were always trying do things to get you off of the crew like stealing your tools and crazy things. I think I gravitated toward the craft end of the business because that was the group that was much more accepting and supportive of what I could do."

Beth Ireland turning crown molding.

Beth remained focused, developing her carpentry skills, and opened up her own shop. Early on she had the fortune of meeting a highly supportive client, who was a professor at Boston University. This one client was so supportive of and excited about what Beth was doing that she opened doors to other clients. Beth claims that all of the work she's done in her career as a woodworker stems from this one client and the community she introduced her to. Early on in her career she also befriended a man who owned a mill, and he took it upon himself to teach her patternmaking and proper use of tools.

Her path into the art of woodturning came out of necessity in 1986 when she needed architectural turning for a job she was doing and couldn't find a turner. She bought a lathe and taught herself how to turn. As a curious and tenacious learner, the wood lathe captured her attention and she developed a business in architectural turning. Her somewhat compulsive need to make, learn, and innovate allowed her to maintain a commercial business in architectural turning while developing her other artistic pursuits. Beth worked with mixed media, turning decorative and sculptural forms and making artist books, and when she turned fifty-two, she was admitted into the sculpture program at Massachusetts College of Art. During this period she immersed herself in the conceptual realm and developed a significant body of sculptural work. The education, experience, and opportunity to work thematically helped her delve deeper into her ideas and personal aesthetic voice. She discovered the benefit of pursuing artist residencies to advance her artistic practice. Beth credits the time and space afforded during residencies, like the Windgate residency at SUNY Purchase College, for the breakthrough moments that culminated in her most developed sculptural concepts.

Beth also credits a friend working in real estate for advising her to buy a house to stabilize her costs of being an artist. She mentored Beth by encouraging her to explore programs to help self-employed people buy houses. Beth bought a triple-decker house, which she says really changed her life by providing rental income and a stable studio space.

"I came to wood because it isn't dependent on other people, and I could have a minimal amount of tools and make things. But really, if I had discovered book making back then, I would be a book artist."

Her life and career are a consummation of many elements; sometimes she will turn two hundred balusters so that she can have the time to make the sculpture she wants to make. Beth doesn't consider it a compromise, because the turning informs the technical and visual aspects of her work.

"Although seemingly tedious or boring, it is not. My work falls in a quirky realm of object making. I have always felt there is not enough craft in art, and not enough art in craft. My graduate professor Judy Haberl taught me about conceptual ideas, and mentored me in the life of an artist, the idea of concept, and art history. I am compelled and interested in materials and how they go together, and I'm really interested in how I can translate an idea I am having into the real world—it doesn't matter if it's through writing, drawing, sculpture...I think you have something inside you that wants to come out in a material world."

She loves to teach and finds it to be an art in itself. Combining teaching and making led to her project "Turning around America," when she left her shop and traveled in a mobile studio (which she also lived in) for a year, with the purpose of teaching as many people as she could how to make simple objects in wood. Beth traveled thirty thousand miles and taught more than three thousand people how to make a tool, whistle, or pen. When she conceived the idea for "Turning around America," she put together a crowd-source fundraiser, which was extremely successful and provided her the funding to outfit a van as her studio and living space.

At the age of forty, Beth discovered that she is severely dyslexic, but she had never been diagnosed. She admits to having struggled through high school and believes she was admitted into college conditionally because her teachers vouched for her. Reflecting upon her life, she notes that she circumvented and adapted to challenges and always knew that she would not thrive in an office but rather a workshop where she "didn't have to fake it."

To support herself, Beth lectures, demonstrates, and teaches at wood turning clubs; runs an architectural turning and carving business; lectures at colleges; and teaches workshops at schools

"Turning around America" mobile workshop (woodworking shop).

such as the Center for Furniture Craftsmanship, Arrowmont School of Arts and Crafts, and Peters Valley School of Craft. Currently, Beth is focused on making all sorts of beautiful and whimsical stringed instruments, and teaching herself how to play them by watching YouTube videos.

Staking out a territory between painting and sculpture, Ron Isaacs's work explores ideas of paradoxical interruptions and metamorphoses. Ron discovered a paper sculpture book at the public library around the age of eleven. He toyed with his paper creations for a while before delving deeper into sculpture. He studied art at Berea College, earning his BA, and then went on to earn his MFA from Indiana University in painting. He painted on canvas until about 1970, when he found a collage element that he wanted to incorporate into a painting. "My father sawed out a piece of wood I could glue it to and attach to the surface

Ron Isaacs

Wood

"Improve Each Shining Hour" c. 2010, 43.5"×29"×2.75". Acrylic on birch plywood construction.

"Flourish" c. 2013, 54.5"×27.5"×3.5". Acrylic on birch plywood construction.

"La Nuit" c. 2009, 37.5"×80.5"×8.5". Acrylic on birch plywood construction.

"Child" c. 2012, 27.5"×25.75"×3.5". Acrylic on birch plywood construction.

of the canvas. I liked that it added another level and dimension to break through the rectangle, and I started sawing myself a few different shapes that I painted and added to the canvas." After about three or four paintings like this, he realized that he didn't need the canvas; he could paint on any shape or form. Moving away from the rectangular picture frame allows Ron to focus on the relief structures. Early on, Ron started creating multiple figure imagery. He entered a piece into an exhibition at Mount St. Joseph University in Cincinnati, Ohio, in the fall of 1972, receiving the first purchase prize in the amount of $2,000. This solidified his decision to pursue a career as a professional artist.

Based on the success, he took a few pieces and traveled to Chicago to gallery shop for a day; he wound up with his first show in Chicago, and one thing led to another. Ron ended up showing with the Monique Knowlton Gallery, resulting in five successful solo exhibitions in New York City over a ten-year span. Over his fifty plus years of being a maker, Ron has shown with a significant

"I'm seventy-four years old, and I can't wait to see what I do next."

"Corvus" c. 2007, 44.25"×35.5"×5.5". Acrylic on birch plywood construction.

number of galleries. "Usually, getting with a gallery is as a result of being a patron of them. They become aware that I'm an artist too, and they wind up inviting me to show with them. It's very gratifying. One gallery I still show with, Snyderman-Works Gallery in Philadelphia, recently celebrated their fiftieth anniversary!"

Despite Ron's successful exhibition record, he realized that it would be difficult for him to depend solely on his artwork to pay the bills. He taught at the college level for thirty-six years, retiring in 2001 from Eastern Kentucky University. "It's an almost ideal situation for an artist. Your basic income is taken care of, and it gives you time to make work. You're expected to be a practicing artist; the teaching feeds the art and the art feeds the teaching."

Ron currently lives and works out of his studio in Richmond, Kentucky. He and his wife are planning a move to Lexington,

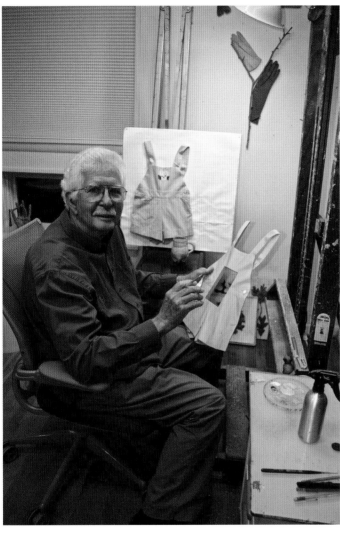

Ron painting a small piece with acrylics.

"There are three levels of success. First is the actual making. That's the most important part, problem solving and creating out of nothing. Secondary is exhibiting the work. It's a measure of success and a fair amount of reward too. Tertiary is selling the work. To me, it's the least important of the three."

Kentucky, where they have been remodeling a two-story town-house with an elevator. The house has a painting studio and a workshop for Ron to work and age in place. "I am proud that I've had an honest to god art career, which is sort of amazing to me… and I've been able to conduct it all from the middle of Kentucky."

Laurie Klein

Photography

"Building the business, changing it, is now as creative for me as shooting."

Laurie Klein began her journey in photography at the age of sixteen, feeling right at home the first time she worked in a darkroom. As a young woman, she says, she felt she was average at everything, but with photography it was different. People seemed to respond to her work; she didn't understand why, but she found the positive reinforcement and the technical and expressive processes very gratifying. She decided to pursue a major in biomedical photography at Rochester Institute of Technology, where she was introduced to infrared camera technology. Infrared is used as a method of creating contrasts for medical research imagery, and Laurie found herself intrigued by the way it captures light so dramatically. She decided to take infrared out of the lab and into the world. She has become one of the leading experts in digital infrared camera technology, utilizing it in her art photography.

During Laurie's sophomore year in college, her bio-medical photography instructor recognized her artistic eye. He set her up

"Eye of the Peacock" c. 2009, 16"×24". Digital infrared.

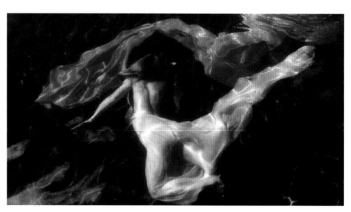

"Water Nymph" c. 2001, 20"×30". Infrared film.

"Fairy Dust" 2010, 16"×24". Digital infrared.

with a semester-long landscape photography project and then encouraged Laurie to change her major to fine arts. Once she entered the arts realm, her intuitive eye was refined, leading to an internship with acclaimed nature photographer Ansel Adams. Adams mentored Laurie in the ways of an art photographer and helped hone her compositional and technical skills.

Soon after graduation she married, had two sons, and divorced. Up until that point photography was merely a hobby for her. It was the need to support her two young sons that led her to explore the possibilities of photography as a career. Starting a commercial wedding photography business, shooting the events in a traditional way, seemed like a perfect solution. It was a juggling

"Bryce and Katie" 2014, 16"×24". Digital infrared.

act at first, but after a couple of years she began connecting different aspects of photography, storytelling, and her own aesthetic sensibilities. At the peak of her business, she had a staff and a schedule of sixty-eight weddings to shoot per year. It took its toll, both physically and emotionally, but she succeeded.

Then, as a way incorporate her creative practice, Laurie began shooting at least one roll of black and white film during each wedding to surprise the bride. She discovered that brides preferred the artful black and white images even more than color photographs. Encouraged by the positive feedback, she increased the number of black and white photographs, which led to greater

"Cabin with Clouds" c. 2014, 16"×24". Digital infrared.

Laurie.

visibility for her as a unique artistic photographer of weddings. Over a few years the nature of her photographic service shifted to black and white art photography.

Laurie quickly understood that her role was not limited to capturing images of groups of people but rather she could tell a story through her lens. Her emotive images captured depth, and her clientele was willing to pay for her talent. Laurie credits taking bold steps toward fulfilling her artistic voice for the success of her unique business model, but most of all for facilitating her development as an artist. By developing a niche in a competitive market, she had the opportunity to go deeper into her practice. Dramatically reducing the number of events she shot annually provided her with more time to develop relationships with clients, which resulted in more meaningful portraiture.

Reaching her midlife she began mentoring young adults, high school, and college age students, sharing with them the technical and storytelling skills she has mastered. From this work she began to evolve her own imagery and develop new themes for visual stories of her own.

"There was a real disconnect for me from being a photographer to being an artist. It took me a few years to connect them. To me it's the spiritual connection to something else—I get out of the way and something comes through me."

Today Laurie supports herself through commissioned work, by teaching immersive experiential photographic workshops at major photography schools across the country, and by writing instructional photography books. She maintains an active social media presence and really enjoys fostering a nurturing community of students. She recently expanded her teaching by offering private online tutorials and online chat groups.

Laurie can certainly cite an interesting trajectory, from an early career in the darkroom with black and white film, to landscape and feminine themes, to storytelling, to digital infrared cameras and digital editing. Laurie is delighted that she can now share her passion and wisdom with others while satisfying her own need to continue to evolve as an artist.

Karen LaFleur is a graphic artist who incorporates computer graphics into her illustrations, stories, and digital animations, allowing her to work in a stunning assortment of formats. From a very young age it was a given that Karen was the artist in her family. Before she could even write, she was creating little story-books with images. "I was actually making books...The characters would say one or two words and I would enhance with drawings; this was at the age of six." Storytelling was a cultural norm for her family of Irish ancestry, and from an early age Karen loved to create imaginative worlds to share with others. Diagnosed with dyslexia, images came much more easily to her than the formation of letters and words.

Karen LaFleur

Mixed Media / Digital

lafleurartworks.com

"Beauty and the Beast" c. 2003, 29"×41". Digital painting with embedded sudden fiction.

Photo credit: Heartland Printworks

"Delany's Garden" c. 2011, 50"×67". Three-dimensional collage.

"Circus" c. 2003, 17"×52". Sequential digital painting with embedded sudden fiction.

"Freeplay" c. 2015, 11"×20". Digital animation.

"Story Star" c. 2015, 10"×17". Digital animation.

Karen holds several degrees, including a BFA in drawing from University of Hartford, a certificate in computer graphics from Rhode Island School of Design, an MA in children's literature from Simmons College, and an MA in illustration from Syracuse University. Her extensive study helped refine and enhance her

"Wings of Lycaeides" c. 2005, 32"×40". Digital painting.

"My partners and friends in the arts have been influential to me, but perhaps the most influential are the puppeteers from Japan that I fell in love with…I learned how the expression of the figure is carried through the toes and fingers in Japanese doll making."

artistic skills, and her studies in literature taught her how to construct a narrative and develop story content. In her work the narrative inspires the visual, and sometimes the story is embedded right into the art.

"I think I was always interested in creating worlds...on Cape Cod I was given the freedom to have my own boat to go explore marshes and explore what nature had to offer. I knew there were worlds inside of worlds, inside of worlds."

Karen married a fellow artist in her early twenties with the dream of moving to New York to make their way as developing artists. The young couple was thrown a curve ball when her husband developed a kidney condition that required a transplant. Because of the diagnosis and how this would affect their lives, they ultimately chose to be close to family on Cape Cod. There they raised their son and established a home and gallery to sell their work from. They committed to working in contemporary art and not in

Photo credit: Marlow Shami

Karen animating still motion figures c. 2015, 7.5"×10".

Photo credit: Marlow Shami

Karen on the computer c. 2014, 3"×6".

the regional themes so popular with the public. Karen continued to evolve as an artist, developing her artistic voice. The setup of her studio was collaborative and varied, showcasing jewelry, clothing, furnishings, contemporary art, and work from artists of the region. As two working artists determined to support their family, the couple explored all sorts of projects clients would bring them, such as welding tractor parts and motorcycle parts, creating window displays for Bloomingdale's, crafting replicas of subway trains, and working with nautical antique dealers. The combination of these efforts provided Karen the platform to explore making large figurative dolls and conversational tableaus. The location of the studio brought in thousands of vacationers over the years, and it was a great way for her to gauge the success of her work by getting immediate and direct feedback from clients.

"You had to be a Jack of all trades because one person would buy this or that. Then you would be commissioned to do this or that, and by the end of the year you actually made a living but not only did you make a living; you had an enormous education with all of the different challenges. It was fun; it really was."

After her first husband's passing she closed the gallery. Today Karen is married to her longtime friend Tommy Simpson. She continues to evolve as an artist working in digital illustrations and narrative and has been developing computer animations to tell new stories.

Her work flow consists of setting goals for projects, and she plans them out utilizing a booklet form for each stage of the process. Typically there will be six to eight projects in the works, with Karen focusing on a priority project. She does, however respond and respect her own need to step away from a project when she reaches a plateau, allowing herself to percolate ideas, moving on to another and maintaining a work flow. Her writing is done in the morning when the words come more easily, and her production work happens in the afternoon and evening. She typically works from eight in the morning until eight at night, and if the work is progressing, she continues on into the evening. Her animations are extremely time consuming and have several components to consider, such as music, story, art, drawings, what will be built, and what will be 3-D animated or 2-D animated. Her planning and persistence are key to the completion of a piece.

Douglas
Peltzman

Ceramics

dougpeltzman.com
instagram.com/dougpeltzman

"Spending my youth on a skateboard taught me discipline and focus, to never give up and embrace failure."

Douglas Peltzman is a studio potter based in New York State. He supports himself and his family through the sale of functional pottery. Doug graduated with his BFA from SUNY New Paltz in 2003, served as a summer assistant under Bruce Dehnert at Peters Valley School of Craft in 2004, worked as a studio technician from 2006 to 2008 at the Hartford Art School, and earned his MFA at Pennsylvania State University. He believes that all of these experiences had an immensely profound impact on the trajectory and success of his choice to be a studio potter. Each one presented different challenges and spawned lifelong relationships. "My partner Pam and I understand and empathize with each other and with the hardships of being a full-time artist. It takes an immense amount of time, energy, and sacrifice to put in long hours in the studio."

Rather than following an academic career, Doug has chosen the path of a full-time maker. Doug prefers this lifestyle—being his own boss, working long hours, and having the freedom to spend time with his two young children. Doug teaches workshops around the country and makes and sells his pots full time, with a steady record of commission work. He is also a founding member of Objective Clay, a collaborative blog and sales gallery maintained and run by a group of eleven different artists, and works hard to promote his work through Facebook and Instagram. "Sharing my process and ideas with collectors and enthusiasts whether through social media or in person is an investment in the future and a connection to a community that I love. The more personal you get with your work and the more understanding you have of your work gives people a story about it. They are not just buying a pot; they are investing in a career."

"Teapot" c. 2015, 5"×6.75"×5.25". Electric fired porcelain, wheel thrown.

"Yunomi Grouping" c. 2015, 3.5"×3.5"×3".
Electric fired black porcelain, wheel thrown.

"Yunomi Grouping" 2015, 3.5"×3.5"×4".
Electric fired porcelain, wheel thrown.

"I feel good about what I make and what I put out in the world. I feel a sense of accomplishment. Our sole income comes from my pottery business, and I have been supporting my family on that income since 2012."

"Jar" c. 2015, 5.75"×6.25"×10.25". Electric fired porcelain, wheel thrown.

Doug working in his studio, c. 2015.

Doug's studio shelving, c. 2015.

A die-hard skater turned potter, Doug pulls inspiration for imagery from observing patterns, compositions, and textures in nature and industry, finding an infinite well of meaning and conceptual material. His imagery is a mash up of bright colors, symbols, familiar marks, and grids, repeated to create intricate graphics alluding to his youth.

Growing up not far from NYC, and not far from the ocean, one can see the influence of skater culture and industrial architecture in Doug's work. Recently he has been looking at early Atari video games for source material. "Some of the forms I make are reminiscent of smoke stacks, old Tupperware cups from the 1980s, Wedgewood and Staffordshire ceramics that I grew up seeing and living with, ancient Mimbres and Jomon pottery, and old metal objects that I find and collect. The paintings and writings of Agnes Martin have also been a major source of inspiration and influence. I love playing with abstraction on the surface of pottery."

"The imagery isn't just looked at; it's touched, and that opens up exciting moments for discovery and surprise. I am always negotiating with function and trying to find a balance between highly crafted utilitarian pots and engaging active objects to look at."

Ellie Richards

Wood

ellie-richards.com
instagram.com/ellieinthewoods

Ellie Richards is a sculptural woodworker currently based out of the Penland School of Crafts in the Blue Ridge Mountains of North Carolina. Her educational path has existed both in and out of academia. She earned her BFA in sculpture from University of Dayton and her MFA from Arizona State University. She has a hunger to improve her craftsmanship and seeks out supplemental learning opportunities via craft programs to achieve the skills to make the work that she wants to make. Her work is playful in nature and explores ideas of regularity and relationships through a rapid and repetitive generation of form.

Ellie attributes much of her success to having supportive parents and being granted the opportunity to be an artist in residence at several craft schools throughout the country. The opportunity to have creative freedom in the studio and build a network with visiting artists allowed her to use her experiences as a springboard into something else.

Photo credit: Mercedes Jelinek

Ellie in the studio.

Holding a position at Penland School of Crafts as a studio coordinator, receiving grants, and selling work allows Ellie the opportunity to apply for grants and plan her next move. She employs a bartering system with other resident artists in order to build her portfolio. Working at Penland has also allowed her to make work that she otherwise would not have the equipment or studio space to make.

Perhaps unsurprisingly, sweeping is an important ritual for Ellie—so much so that she started a new series of work focused on the broom. "Sometimes I clean too much and use it as a way

"Crusaders: Crew 1/9" c. 2013, 24"×48"×6". Band saw carved, then painted.

"Upside Down Bench" c. 2015, 24"×36"×13". Found wood, carved legs, paint and wax finish.

"It seems being an artist will always be about learning to create and grow into a better version of myself and my work, and that is something I'm totally okay with."

to procrastinate from doing another task. One of my favorite things to do is sharpen my colored pencils. It always puts me in a positive mind-set and allows me to move forward cheerfully."

Gaining inspiration from walks in the woods, exploring thrift stores, and using time stuck on airplanes to create impossible ideas, Ellie's work explores the whimsy of taking an everyday useful object and giving it a life and personality, at times deeming it useless. Sometimes she will create quick gestural sketches of her plans, but in general, Ellie works reactively with the found objects and materials.

"I don't think an aesthetic voice is something that comes by trying but rather by doing the things that bring the most satisfaction in visual and conceptual ways. Curating and editing ideas is a skill that grows with time and could be the key to having continuity be evident in the work."

"Technicolor Stacks" c. 2013, 18"×3"×3". Band saw boxes, acrylic paint.

"Polychrome Dining Table" c. 2015, 36"×48"×96". Oxidized cherry, acrylic paint.

Kristal Romano's work plays with ideas of cultural value. She creates primarily small-scale and wearable sculptures of precious metals combined with ordinary found objects. Responding to her environment and everyday experiences, she creates situations in which objects are altered or detached from their natural function. Kristal is drawn to metals such as copper, brass, bronze, as well as the fine jewelry metals, silver and gold, because they are loaded with intrinsic, aesthetic, and cultural value. Captivated by the interplay of adornment, scale, and nontraditional materials, the found objects she uses are typically more commonplace, but circulate through contemporary culture as signifiers of importance, worth, or usefulness of something.

Kristal Romano

Fine Metals

kristalromano.com
instagram.com/kristalromano

"Large Enamel Necklace" 18". 14k gold filled, torch fired enamel on copper, steel with a gloss enamel finish.

"Large Enamel Earrings" 2.5" long, 1.25" across. 14k gold filled, torch fired enamel on copper, steel with a gloss enamel finish.

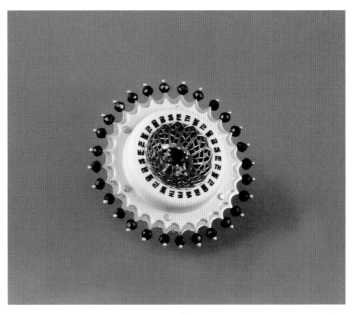

"Birth Control Dial Brooch" 3"×3"×.5". Sterling silver, brass, garnet, plastic dial from birth control pack.

Humor is an important element in Kristal's work. Sometimes her works appear idiosyncratic and quirky; at other times, they seem like typical by-products of American superabundance and marketing. Levity allows viewers to enter her work on one level, but with more time spent, additional layers of meaning unfold to facilitate a deeper understanding of value. Much of Kristal's work has heavy feminist undertones.

"I guess it's my values as far as fighting for what's fair or finding validation in a lot of things. The birth control pieces are speaking about ideas of value because they're made of precious metals and precious stones, so you know it's a precious thing that other people in the world have a lot of big opinions on. By making it something valuable, there's a duality in that it's still out of reach of the people that need it or want it. It was something that I could no longer afford to have, so this was like my way of calling attention to this injustice."

Her personality is quiet and subdued generally, but she often plays stand-up comedy on her phone while she's working in the studio; that humor seeps into her themes. Her snarky sense of humor shines through in her work in the form of satire and plays on words. She likes to have a sense of humor about serious things. "It's a good way to enter a subject, no matter how difficult a situation is. It makes me realize how much I'm like my dad. My dad can't deal with things without making a joke. He's the worst guy to have in the room if someone is sick."

"Credit Card Ring" ring size 7. Sterling silver, credit card.

Kristal's goal is to have people recognize found pieces and understand the subject, and her quirkiness gives her work a twist to bring you back to what is serious. Her subject matter reflects her own life and story, often coincidentally lining up with some bigger stories in the news. Reflecting on a series of rings sculpted from credit cards, Kristal reflects, "With [my] credit card pieces, they're most effective as rings because it's 'the diamond is forever but in this economy your debt is forever.'"

While attending college at Kutztown University, Kristal realized that jewelry would always be a part of what she did. She didn't understand at the time that one could actually make a career out of it. She thought she would be a painting major until she met Kiki Adams, who encouraged her to work three-dimensionally. "[Kiki's] personality was so powerful and active with the students, and that was a huge influence to me. I loved that she was a woman who dove right into working and encouraged other women to learn to weld."

After her time at Kutztown, Kristal spent a summer at Peters Valley School of Craft in New Jersey as a resident assistant. Another resident artist encouraged her to apply for a job with high-end New York City jeweler Ten Thousand Things. "This was a completely serious full-time job making jewelry for celebrities that were in magazines, and at the same time I was just the one working in the back. It was their brand; I was just one of the makers."

> "Jewelry making is so fulfilling. Stimulating in one aspect and then just really fun and full of joy in the other. You're just adorning things that are pretty!"

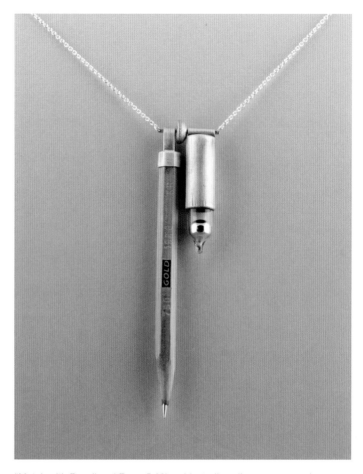

"Metalsmith Pencil and Eraser" 18k gold, sterling silver, mercury, glass, wood.

Kristal found that working as a bench jeweler provided her with experience to hone her skills and understand how to work with clients to bring their ideas to life, but she found this was not nearly as satisfying as making her own work. Fortunately, her time as a summer resident provided her with a network that gave her many opportunities in her career. "It gives you permission to do what you want to do, more than other perches. It also provides the encouragement to keep looking and doing it and finding ways to do it after being there. It's not a long-term arrangement, so it pushes you to the next thing and figuring out what that might be."

She soon applied for a grant through the Massachusetts Museum of Contemporary Art. "When I found out about that grant through MASS-MoCA it seemed like another way to continue that similar atmosphere and similar approach to learning, making and having a community but in a new place that's surrounded by a

The artist at work at her bench.

contemporary art museum. It is a group of people that are coming from all disciplines like writers and musicians in addition to sculptors and painters and people who make jewelry like me. That opportunity is awesome."

Last year, Kristal tested the waters with her jewelry line at the American Craft Council Show in Baltimore and unfortunately watched her bank account disappear. "You try and you learn a lot every time you do. You try to make the right decisions. It's now me on my own, and so it's not perfect yet and money may not be spent as wisely as it should be, but I know next time it will be better and every time it will grow like that."

She recently moved to Massachusetts, dramatically resetting her lifestyle. To aid her transition, she began teaching at Montclair State University, requiring a long commute of four hours or more multiple times each week. "I use the time in the car to organize the class and my head or to have those aha moments where I come up with a great new piece, then work out the steps as I'm driving along…and then I miss my exit but that's okay! I just turn around!"

Judith Schaechter

Glass

judithschaechter.com

Judith Schaechter has managed to create incredible works of art using a material called "flash glass" to build narrative imagery in large-scale stained glass panels. Her creations are centered on the idea of transforming the wretched into the beautiful—say, unspeakable grief, unbearable sentimentality or nerve-wracking ambivalence, and representing it in such a way that is inviting and safe.

Judith graduated with her BFA from the Rhode Island School of Design's glass program in 1983. She originally studied painting but instantly fell in love with glass after taking an elective course; she knew that it was what she wanted to pursue for the rest of her life. She describes working with glass as unlike most raw materials because glass is extremely attractive to begin with, before the artist even touches it. Judith likes to "manipulate it, stretch it, transform it and distort it in unnatural ways. I like to see what possibilities lie in mating difficult emotional ideas with sensuous but cruel materials." And through technique and concept, she's successfully worked within an ancient art/craft as a modern artist.

Judith also found herself attracted to the brief history of the advancement of glass, while being intimidated by the lengthy,

Photo credit: Dom Episcopo

"The Battle of the Carnival and Lent" c. 2011, 56"×56". Stained glass, cut, sandblasted, engraved, painted, stained, and fired, cold paint and assembled with copper foil.

"The Birth of Eve" c. 2013, 57"×31". Stained glass, cut, sandblasted, engraved, painted, stained, and fired, cold paint and assembled with copper foil.

"Horse Accident" c. 2015, 33"×45". Stained glass, cut, sandblasted, engraved, painted, stained, and fired, cold paint and assembled with copper foil.

"I like a lot of resistance. I like cold, hard, sharp, vicious stuff to fight with—I dislike compliance! Perhaps I want to punish it for being so pretty when I sometimes feel so ugly."

deep, and complicated history of painting. For Judith, glass, this labor-intensive medium, helped her moved through her self-diagnosed attention deficit disorder. One could describe her process as contemporary drawings in glass using traditional techniques in use for centuries. The imagery is mainly engraved into layers of glass using only black and yellow paints, and all other colors are achieved from the flash glass pieces which are soldered together using copper foil and lead.

Much of Judith's work is improvised and made without prior plans or sketches. She doesn't have clear narratives in mind and tries to be deliberately vague, but she finds the beauty of glass to be the perfect counterpoint to ugly and difficult subjects. "A radiant, transparent, glowing figure is not the same as a picture of a figure (which reflects light). It's a blatant reference to holiness or some type of 'supernatural' state of being." She sees her figures—although they're meant to be ordinary people doing ordinary things—as having much in common with old medieval windows of saints and martyrs. They seem to be caught in a transitional moment when despair becomes hope or darkness becomes inspiration.

"Odalisque" c. 2015, 24"×33". Stained glass, cut, sandblasted, engraved, painted, stained, and fired, cold paint and assembled with copper foil.

With the initial financial support of her parents, Judith was able to establish a studio in her home in Philadelphia. This allowed her to work without significant financial pressure. Judith sells her artwork through the Claire Oliver Gallery in Chelsea, New York, in addition to doing adjunct teaching for several art schools such as University of the Arts, Pennsylvania Academy of Fine Arts, and the New York Academy. Though there was no singular moment that led Judith to become an artist, she acknowledges that she benefitted from early recognition from curators Susanne Frantz and Michael Monroe, who gave her opportunities to exhibit work and be featured in publications.

While many artists find it difficult to focus in a studio at home, Judith finds that she likes the seclusion because she can work freely through the medium without interruption. Her work flow requires twelve hours of free time to have three hours of productive time in the studio, which mostly occur in the early hours of the morning.

Judith finds inspiration in improvisation and spontaneity. She occasionally will sketch ideas, input the imagery into Photoshop, and then play with it, relying on gut and intuition. A work's image

Judith soldering in her studio.

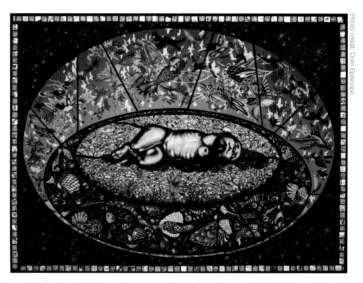

"Three Tiered Cosmos" c. 2015, 30"×40". Stained glass, cut, sandblasted, engraved, painted, stained, and fired, cold paint and assembled with copper foil.

can be made up of one or two hundred drawings. Then this black and white image will come to life when working with the colored glass. Judith's attraction to glass has multiple layers. "First, it is beautiful—light being transmitted through color...Well, doesn't everyone like that? But mostly it is technical. Ironically, I found my artistic voice was liberated by technical restrictions and by losing the inhibitions I associated with the high seriousness of the classical painting tradition."

James Schriber has never been completely comfortable calling himself an artist because he never thought about becoming an artist and believes he ended up being a maker by default. He has led a successful career by making commercial and studio furniture.

James was born into a family of contractors; his father owned a large commercial contracting business. As a teenager he developed a work ethic by learning to how to run a crew by working with his father. As the youngest son in his family, James was often left to his own devices, with freedom and parental support to pursue his interests. He really had no scholarly ambitions as a young man. In fact, he suspects if he were in school today, a

James Schriber

Wood

jamesschriber.com

Photo credit: John Kane

"Two-Door Cabinet." Cherry with paint.

"Given my somewhat limited talent I have done pretty well. I think there are some people I went to school with, colleagues, who had much more natural talent than I did. I recognized that early on, and in some ways I have achieved just as much if not more than a lot of them have. You do the best you can with what you have."

"Two-Door Cabinet." Cherry.

learning deficit would be detected. Fortunately, he discovered an aptitude for making objects by first repairing bicycles and then building motorcycles, scooters, and cars.

For James, making things with his hands was at the core of his artistry. When he discovered that it was possible to make things with some intelligence behind them, he decided to look for a school that had a design program. He applied and was accepted into Goddard College, where he would learn about design and architecture. He quickly found himself immersed in a very creative environment with inspiring teachers and mentors. He then went to Philadelphia to work with Dan Jackson, who was completely supportive and "a fantastic teacher." Later, he attended Boston University for the artisanry program. There he found himself among

"Dining Table." Walnut.

"I pursued something I didn't even know was a possibility growing up. I pursued a lifestyle that appealed to me as I was maturing. I don't feel as if I have made any sacrifices…I have always enjoyed working."

"Magazine Tables." Wood and aluminum.

colleagues and friends who became the emerging artists represented by the fledgling galleries showing studio furniture in the late 1970s and early 1980s in the Boston area.

"I would like to think it was because of my hard work but really some of it was because of my associations. They were all lucky breaks…I learned how to work hard in my father's company. I always enjoyed the idea of hard work. And the environment at Goddard was very hard working. People were working all the time…I have always enjoyed pushing myself."

When he started out professionally, he worked with an architect and a contractor and established a commercial side to his business. James recognized early on that it wasn't possible for him to make enough work alone. He simply couldn't pursue the

"Console Table." Cerused ash.

"Console Table." Cerused ash.

commercial and artistic aspects of the work without help. Over the last eight to ten years, since the gallery market has been greatly reduced, he has put a lot more energy into the commercial end of his business. In addition to making studio furniture, he offers architectural millwork for designers and architects for big projects. This commercial aspect has been the sustaining element and key to the success of his business.

James is very clear about who he is and how he works primarily through commissions, not so much self-motivated the way some artists work. He enjoys outside stimulus to set criteria around designs. He typically works with a client and listens to what they want, sits at the drawing table, and then moves to the bench and

"Bench." Cherry.

gets to work. Sometimes this requires a return to the drawing table until a design is resolved. He admits it was a bit of a struggle in college to be surrounded by artists who displayed distinct styles right from the start. Today, as an accomplished and mature designer and maker, James credits much of his success to his adaptability. In fact, his ability to respond to his clients' criteria and ability to design in different styles has been his key to customer satisfaction and a continuous flow of work.

James recognizes that there are easier ways to make a living, but he has remained interested and engaged in his business because it requires so many different skill sets. "There are aspects of being a salesman and a self-promoter but you have to have the craft skills, and you have to be an entrepreneur…I like making a business out of it…Perhaps I would have done better by pursuing limited production runs over the art gallery aspect. I think I would have been better suited for that, but I didn't even know about it at the time."

With no regrets James has enjoyed making a business out of all of his skills, engaging in a variety of jobs, not just standing behind his work bench all day putting pieces of wood together. He still enjoys moving from one thing to another, which keeps him interested. James's work has been featured in major publications in contemporary furniture design.

Biba Schutz

Fine Metals

bibaschutz.com

"Taking the time away from working in my studio for a month to just work in another way was an unbelievable gift."

Biba Schutz has built a solid career as a metalsmith. As a little girl Biba sensed that the way she played was different from the other children around her. She loved making things and spent a lot of time drawing and fantasizing about living the life of an artist. Biba is convinced that she must have heard a story about an artist's life in elementary school, because she doesn't know how else she could have fantasized about living in a Paris garret in second grade.

Biba earned a BA from American University and then studied printmaking at Pratt Institute and fibers at Instituto de Allende in Mexico. While at the Instituto she had second thoughts about moving from the drawing board to the loom because it seemed far too structured and similar. Resolute that she wanted to work three-dimensionally, Biba left the fibers program. Graphic design allowed her to build her skills while earning a living, but she felt a sense of dissatisfaction with two-dimensional work, leading her to work with various materials before settling on the idea of making jewelry and three-dimensional objects. Practicality and entrepreneurial perspectives convinced her that making and selling jewelry was a more plausible way to make a living than paper-making, and that it could help her transition from graphic design to studio art.

Biba spent four to five years teaching herself how to make jewelry as an independent graduate study. It wasn't easy, and required her to make her own tools because she didn't know they could in fact be purchased. The process of figuring out fabrication techniques on her own was difficult but beneficial. Biba believes having to figure out how to make what she imagined without any

Photo credit: Ron Bozko

"Wyred" c. 2016, 4.3"×3.8"×2". Steel, sterling silver.

"Tillie's Time" c. 2016, 2.25"×2.25"×1". Oxidized sterling silver, Herkimer diamond, handmade flax asper, adhesives, steel.

"Turning" c. 2014, 4"×3.5"×1.25". Sterling silver, mica, steel, Herkimer diamond.

established path allowed her to develop her own unique style. Her investment in learning, and her later discovery that professional jewelry making tools could be purchased, helped advance her work technically (although her self-made hammers, chasing, and repoussé tools are still in use and quite important to her practice). Biba's background in graphic design taught her precision, great hand-eye coordination, and most importantly the ability to translate what she envisions into physical form. "As a graphic designer problem solving is very pertinent in the process. I use that in my creative process even now."

Biba's love for color is evident in her graphics work and drew her into working with anodized aluminum, a metal she had tactile and visual history with. Her early pursuits with aluminum allowed her to manipulate and fabricate jewelry and vessels, attempting to utilize basketry techniques to create three-dimensional forms. Her next leap forward came when she heeded her friend's advice to work with silver or bronze or copper. "As soon as I switched, it broke open for me. I had so many more opportunities."

During a workshop with Charles Lewton-Brain she learned to approach metal as a plastic, honoring its potential to take any form, to move and to flow.

Biba says that's what she loves about metal: it is unlimited. It starts as a nugget but she can shape the metal and create forms that are sometimes unimaginable. She starts with a plan but lets the material guide her. She changes an idea or drawing to fit how the metal moves.

Challenges have been a driving force for Biba's artistic pursuits; she focuses her attention, meeting these challenges head on and problem solving. There is a very clear sense of adventure and exploration in her work. "I spend more time being Biba Schutz than anything else. So I have to be interested and engaged and challenged to keep that going. To keep it fresh…Challenging yourself and going deep is not what you call fun, but the gratification is priceless! To feel like you have done that and then for people to recognize it is so gratifying. It works both ways."

Biba's studio is located in a commercial building in New York City where she employs multiple assistants. Typically, her assistants are classically or academically trained metalsmiths. Sometimes the work can be a little challenging, but it provides them with wonderful learning opportunities. She makes work in editions, but more than half of her output is one of a kind. For Biba, her sculptural jewelry has to work on the body, and it is meant to be worn. Typically her work is made of silver, bronze, bone, and more recently, blown glass, a shift inspired by one of her assistants.

Biba's new experimentation with glass led her to take an artist residency at Corning Glass in New York. It has led to a wonderful new series that has been shown in three museums. Incorporating glass into her metal jewelry has been extremely difficult, but it has been very engaging for Biba and she plans to pursue another residency. "The new work is different but what is consistent is that…there is a place to hide in the work. That is very consistent."

Half of the income for Biba's business derives from wholesale gallery accounts, and the other half is from retail fairs. Her income

"Ruffle Cuffs" c. 2016. Sterling silver, copper.

"Puckered Up" c. 2014, 9"×9"×1.5". Rosé glass, sterling silver.

"Some of my customers
have grown alongside
me...I have retail
customers that are
personal friends. Some
have been so loyal and
have so much of my work
that it is embarrassing."

"Over n Over" c. 2014, 7.5"×7.5"×1". Bronze necklace forged and
constructed.

"Charlotte Russe" c. 2016, 13"×10"×10". Steel, copper, bronze.

"Black Score" c. 2015, 9.5"×8.5"×1.3". Black borosilicate glass, cut, sandblasted, oxidized sterling silver.

from retail shows helps, as gallery sales are simply not enough to support the overhead costs of her NYC studio. She has had her studio for more than twenty years, just about as long as she has been married, and has a deep commitment to both her artistry and partnership. Over the years, she has made great friends and has enjoyed a community of makers, gallery owners, and collectors.

Joyce performing at Common Ground on the Hill, a roots, social justice, and arts festival in Maryland.

Joyce J. Scott

Mixed Media & Fibers

Joyce J. Scott was a latch-key kid who grew up in Baltimore in a second-floor apartment. She would come home from school, do her homework, have a snack, and then make art. Her mother, Elizabeth T. Scott, was a nationally known fiber artist who encouraged Joyce to lead a creative life. She taught her beadwork, stitching, and weaving, which gave Joyce the basic skills for her work. Joyce attended a demonstration school, which served as an experimental learning community for student teachers to try various teaching methods. As a result, Joyce was exposed to a lot of advanced and creative ways to educate students in the arts.

In 1976 Joyce went to Haystack Mountain School of Crafts for their bicentennial celebration, where she learned the peyote stitch. This was a significant change to her practice. For her it meant she no longer needed a loom or fabric; she only needed a needle,

"Lewd #1" c. 2013, 11"×21"×6". Hand-blown Murano glass processes with beads, wire, and thread.

"Success is not a one-prong fork. There are many fingers coming out of that hand."

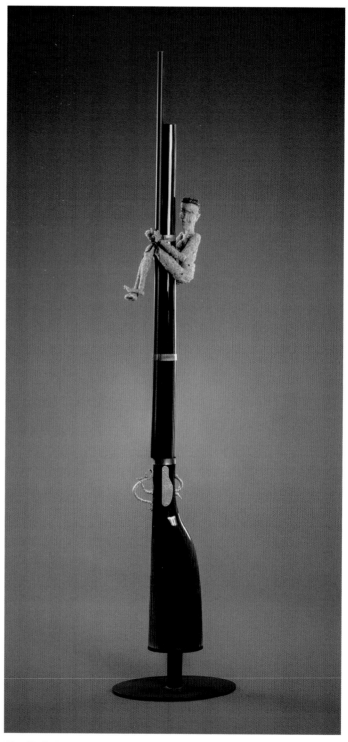

"Sex Traffic" c. 2014. Hand-blown Murano glass metal, beads, thread, leather.

"Lover's Necklace" c. 2005. Beads, thread, wire.

"[My inspiration] came from my mom and my dad and those who were conscientious about helping me evolve as a true human…as a human being who understood that I was on a quest and that I would lose by not going after it, that my light would not be as bright if I didn't go after it. That's success for me. I'm still fabulous!"

thread, and beads. "This technique means that now I could work flat, or sculptural. Because it doesn't have flammable material, it also means I can apply it to other materials."

Joyce earned her BA in art education from the Maryland Institute College of Art. "Going to art school meant that I had to face the responsibility of my choices and the cost of my creativity." After school, she began student teaching and found that to be a miserable experience. Like a true hippie, Joyce and her girlfriends took off to Mexico. "My parents were both sharecroppers, picking cotton and tobacco. They never would have imagined that I would have the gumption to go off to a foreign country to find myself. I'm grateful to the courage that my parents had to allow me to do these things so I could follow my pursuit of this holy art grail or this golden ring I've been going after."

Joyce spent a year in Mexico earning her MFA. When she returned to the United States, she took a job as a drug counselor.

"War Woman I" c. 2014, 30"×20"×20". African sculpture, dice, glass/plastic beads, thread, wire, cast glass guns.

"Obama/Virgen de Guadelupe" c. 2000–2012. Screen-print, hand painting, collage, embossed paper, ceramic charms, prayer cards.

"I was not a drug abuser, though most drug counselors have been in their past. My modality was using art, so we painted murals and made objects in clay. I saw the very worst of humanity and people who have done the very worst of everything to get their drugs." After that experience, Joyce knew that she would never work for anyone ever again.

Joyce was in theatre for several years. She was a member of a group called the Thunder Thigh Revue, who traveled across the nation and the UK and put on political and social comedies. "I was told when I was serious about pursuing music that I would have to stop the visual art, that I must commit completely. It was a good choice, but I do performance and my studio art. Perhaps I missed out on a TV show or a record deal, but I had to lose something to get something else. Now, I don't have to choose!" Performance art has allowed Joyce to see the world and get paid for it. For years, she spent a lot of time traveling to teach, give critiques, lecture, and do performances.

"Oh Hell No!" c. 2007. Peyote stitched glass beads, blown glass, wire, thread.

In 2016, Joyce was awarded a MacArthur fellowship in recognition of her contribution to the arts. She currently maintains two houses. One house serves as her dwelling and a small office, and her other house serves as her studio space, located in the Station North Arts and Entertainment District of Baltimore. Her district is home to a forthcoming arts space called The Motor House, where Joyce will be the first artist in residence. She pieces her income together by selling work through two galleries and doing some trunk shows. In particular she does a Christmas sale in her neighborhood every year. "I do the Christmas sale because it's a way for me to thank all of those friends who have supported me since I was sixteen and who can't pay ten thousand dollars for a necklace. I not only make money, but people from elementary school come see me. It stems from that entrepreneurship that many artists have. I have a secondary market where I can make objects that are not about something social or political, but just pretty that someone can easily afford."

Staying true to herself means making work about topics that are uncomfortable for people. Her work is provocative. She understands that there are some pieces that will only be purchased by a collector or institution, and not by people who like to have beautiful pictures in their home. Joyce finds personal success in the fact that she made a career as an artist who explored difficult themes honestly and without compromise.

Wyatt Daglã Severs realized at a very young age that he could draw better than the other kids around him. It made sense to him that being a maker would be a good career choice. Early on, Wyatt thought he wanted to be a teacher. Diagnosed with dyslexia, he wanted to give back and help kids like himself. Although he can't be a grade school teacher, he is able to work with children teaching them woodworking skills.

When Wyatt isn't riding his bike or attending concerts, he's in his studio. He remodeled an art guild building in Kentucky and, in exchange, has affordable rent on his studio space. As a part of the guild he has the opportunity to teach kids' classes and one-on-one workshops to students with special needs. Wyatt

Wyatt Daglã Severs

Wood

wyattsevers.com

"Chair Won" c. 2009, 36"×20"×17". Maple, mahogany, bent plywood, copper, silver, Danish oil.

"Day Table" c. 2015, 31"×25.75"×6.5". Cherry, maple, milk paint, Danish oil.

makes his income from these workshops, making Christmas ornaments, various landscaping and stonework jobs, and commissions. "I choose to work every day, all day. I travel a lot, which means being away from my family and friends. I don't like being away; I'm a country boy at heart, but I love to travel."

Wyatt loves teaching because he loves seeing other people, especially kids, become interested in making. "I feel successful when I'm teaching kids and they have a great time. I guess success also means paying the bills and being alive...I'd love to break $100,000 a year, but I'm a long ways away from that." Wyatt finds himself inspired by Utah Phillips, an American folk singer who sings about human rights. "I don't read very much, so I listen to his stories about history. He passes history on in words, so maybe I can pass stories down visually for those who can't hear them."

"A Given Shape" c. 2008, 20"×83"×17". Princess wood, poplar, plywood, polyurethane.

"Day Table (detail)" c. 2015, 31"×25.75"×6.5". Cove cut, routering, marquetry.

Wyatt's work is thoughtfully crafted with immense attention to detail. He studied with Stephen Proctor, from whom he learned that a lot comes from trial and error but that making meticulous mathematical drawings is helpful. Wyatt works to create furniture and vessels that are of aesthetic beauty, with great attention to technical skill. Because he did not go to college in the subject, he is unhindered by academic influences and is able to move through the medium with an open mind, giving homage to history and human interaction with the world.

Through summer assistantships and artist residencies, Wyatt has gained a uniquely vast education. He's studied at schools

"My job is like being a big kid. I get to hang out in a clubhouse with cool tools!"

Wyatt preparing to set up his work made during a yearlong residency at Arrowmont School of Arts and Crafts.

Photo credit: James Justin Roberts

Wyatt turning a piece of natural edge green oak.

with programs that introduce you to various working artists in creative atmospheres, including John C. Campbell Folk School, Anderson Ranch, Arrowmont, Peters Valley School of Craft, and Penland School of Crafts, and has traveled as far as New Zealand to apprentice with Graeme Priddle.

Shawn Sheehy is a Chicago-based book artist and designer. For him there isn't a singular moment to becoming an artist. It was longer trajectory that began with growing up in a home with parents who are makers. His mother makes clothing and his father makes furniture. Shawn's artistry came together gradually by earning three degrees. First he headed in the direction of theater and education. Then he gradually pursued a degree in design. Then by happenstance he stumbled upon the book and paper arts program at Columbia College. The richness of this program gave him a path that he was totally passionate about. This was his commitment moment, in 1997, just beyond thirty years of age. He considers himself to have been a bit of a wanderer prior to deciding to become a book artist.

As a child working alongside his parents, who were making dimensional things, he spent a lot of time in his dad's woodshop, carving and whittling away at scraps of wood, thinking dimensionally and sculpturally. "That was very serious groundwork, although utterly unstructured."

Working as a designer of sculptural books made a lot of sense to Shawn because books provide him the perfect avenue to work sculpturally. He has to engineer all the parts, the work can be easily shown, and it can fold away within a book structure.

Shawn credits graduate school as one of the most important opportunities to shape his career. The opportunity to make unhindered work, to explore personal expression while building a professional network and presenting work at an elevated level of

Shawn Sheehy

Book Arts
shawnsheehy.com

Photo credit: Julia Stotz

"A Pop-Up Field Guide to North American Wildflowers" c. 2011, 9"×6"×6.5". Artist book. Commercial cardstock, letterpress, construction.

"Hesperana" c. 2010, 15"×.5"×7". Pop-up folio. Handmade paper, letterpress, construction.

"Welcome to the Neighborwood: A Pop-Up Book of Animal Architecture" c. 2003. 15"×8"×9". Artist book. Handmade paper, letterpress, construction.

exhibition, taught him about the field. Living in Chicago has also brought him advantages. The city has a culture for books and print and a seminal book arts culture. The central location makes for easy travel and facilitates shipping of printed goods; opportunities abound. He has never been married or really been focused on building a family and credits having a lot of solitary time to focus on his work as very self-fulfilling and important to his artistic practice. However, now that he is middle-aged, he recognizes that he has spent twenty-five years building his career, to some

"Beyond the Sixth Extinction: A Fifth Millennium Bestiary" c. 2007, 14.25"×8"×10.25". Artist book. Handmade paper, letterpress, construction.

degree at the expense of interpersonal relationships, and is starting to tilt his head about the topic.

Shawn supports himself as a working artist through four different channels. He built a freelance graphic design business first, as a temporary worker. Over the years he has fostered a relationship with the Chicago Symphony Orchestra, producing their promotional material and posters, and for the past few years works has worked on-site once a week. This provides a steady stream of income so he knows the mortgage will be paid. He makes one of a kind structural books and has recently gone deeper into book making, designing print editions for the publishing world. As his reputation continues to build, he has been

offered teaching opportunities at craft schools and centers who offer book arts courses. Shawn moves forward with this four-pronged model, and as his artist books have become more substantial he has been able to allocate more time to this endeavor. In March 2015, he published the children's book *Welcome to the Neighborhood*.

Shawn lives a simple life with low overhead. It is only in the last five years that he purchased a car and a home in an up and coming West Chicago. The house is nine hundred square feet, with living space downstairs and a perfect studio upstairs. He has a large garden and loves growing flowers and food in an urban setting. At this point, Shawn feels successful because he

View of the studio.

"It kind of tickles all my brain centers, creative, tactile, and produces the right balance of right brain–left brain interplay all of the time."

has been able to create a balanced life and is confident that he can support himself as a working artist. "Knowing that there is always opportunity for me to move up to the next interesting thing and knowing that I have the artistic skill and some luck in trying to cultivate the opportunities to work...I'm feeling successful about that."

In graduate school Shawn learned to record his ideas in journals. He spends a lot of time drawing to figure out the engineering and structure of his books. A lot of the recording of conceptual ideas is done on his phone because it is always on hand. He credits graphic design training for helping him develop critical editing skills to analyze the content, composition, and intent in the work. "A good chunk of the time I have to think really hard and work really hard to develop a concept. A lot of the time I don't have to think at all. I work with the X-ACTO knife and listen to an audio-book...I try to keep all the thinking for the morning...I'm best before lunch and work on production in the afternoon and evening."

In terms of content, the underlying theme in his books is environmental advocacy and the delicate balance of ecosystems. Shawn has combined his education, engineering, design, and storytelling skills to create a career as a book artist and paper engineer, and considers himself an advocate of the natural world.

The notion that things can represent ideas has inspired a lifelong artistic practice for Missy Stevens. She remembers teaching herself how to embroider and then how to sew when she was little, which she enjoyed. But it took her some time as a young adult to even consider a career or life as an artist, partly because she began college at the age of seventeen and wasn't ready. Missy recalls feeling really disinterested in her program of study, and she decided to drop out of college to take time to figure things out.

By taking six years off to work and mature, Missy was able to determine what she really enjoyed doing—and that was working with fabric. She searched for a school that focused on fibers, and attended Boston University's program in artisanry. Missy says that the most important lesson she learned then was that hand skills are as important as mind skills to make art, and she credits professor Dorian Zachai with opening her eyes to what making things, making art, could be.

She also spent many years living and working beside her ex-husband Tommy Simpson. She describes that period in her life as very productive but she and Tommy were both immersed in making art all of the time. "It wasn't really that he was mentoring but that he was supportive of me doing this work. He also saw me as an artist, so that was one fewer person that I had to convince." And naturally, the business of art was their livelihood.

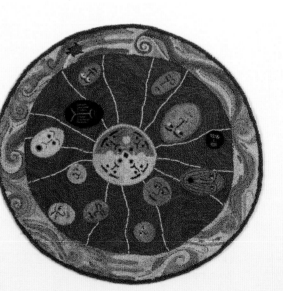

Photo credit: Brad Stanton

"How the River Works" c. 2014, 14"×15"×1". Fiber and beads, loop pile embroidery.

"I think there's just a point where a piece has to be finished. It's a really spongy kind of area but I do my best… I'm looking for them to have some spark inside of them, some magic when they're finished."

"Spring Garden" c. 2012, 15"×11"×2". Fiber, buttons, loop pile embroidery.

For Missy, fiber offers a friendly, accessible, familiar feeling in a cozy kind of way that she's drawn to. She especially enjoys making small-scale works. "There's an intimacy to it and then there's a sort of familiar resonance of all the fabric things we've had in our lives, that we wear every day, that we sleep under…It has a really powerful connection."

Missy has shown in some of the most influential contemporary craft galleries, where her work landed in significant private collections. Because she earned gallery representation, she can now work at her own pace, taking the time needed to complete her thread paintings.

When it comes to her studio practice, she is often presented with opportunities to exhibit in shows that have specific themes

"Protective Garment" c. 2011, 15"×17"×3". Fiber, beads, loop pile and other embroidery.

that push her in new directions; but when she doesn't have a thematic challenge, she creates one. Recently, she challenged herself to create one new piece a month, and found that having a deadline was very helpful because she was continually starting new projects and a rhythm was sustained.

Missy's thread paintings require a very tedious and meticulous process. She draws inspiration from dream sequences, and although she has compositions in mind when she begins a project, she likes to respond to the work and explore color as it comes together, which means she often makes changes or adds elements along the way.

She is very grateful to her father, who was always extremely supportive of her artistic practice, providing a financial cushion as well as materials. He played a role of sponsor and collaborator in her life. There was a phase in which she used to weave rugs out of old clothing, Missy remembers, and all she had to do was tell her father that she was working in corduroy and he would set about collecting material for her projects. She fondly recounts her father showing up with a trailer filled with three hundred pair of corduroy pants, destined to be torn up and repurposed into a woven rug. The support of her father and of her former spouse

"Deep and Light" c. 2009, 6"×6"×6". Fiber, polymer clay, loop pile embroidery, coiling, felting detail.

Missy's studio.

Missy's hands stitching.

provided a comfortable space for her to explore her techniques and ideas in her work.

Partly because of the enormous amount of time it takes to create one of her thread paintings and the physical toll the repetitive motion has imposed on her hands, Missy has gravitated toward different media and has recently enjoyed working in clay for the better part of a year. She has two studio spaces in her home in western Connecticut, one for fiber and one for clay. Although she still feels like a beginner in the realm of clay, she loves the open-ended possibilities of working in it.

Mara Superior, a native New Yorker, has been absorbing art and culture since her childhood in Manhattan. A visit to Chinatown as a little girl sparked her fascination with color, text, and unusual visuals. As a teen she attended the High School of Art and Design and lived several blocks from the Metropolitan Museum of Art. She studied drawing, painting, printmaking, and art history at Pratt Institute and the Hartford Art School, and earned a BFA from the University of Connecticut, Storrs. In 1990 Mara was awarded a National Endowment for the Arts Visual Arts Fellowship, and her work is featured in museums and major collections.

Mara Superior

Ceramics
marasuperiorart.com

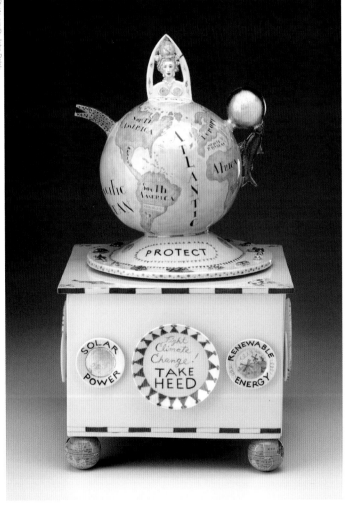

"Homage to Science/Protect the Planet" c. 2012, 11"×11"×24". Slab built high fired porcelain, painted with ceramic underglazes and oxides, gold leaf, tin globe feet.

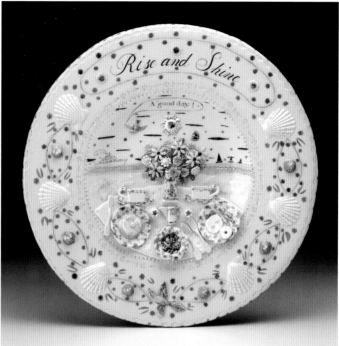

"Rise and Shine" c. 2014, 16" dia. Hand built, high fired porcelain, wall relief sculpture, painted with ceramic underglazes and oxides, gold leaf.

Mara began using porcelain in graduate school at the University of Massachusetts, Amherst. She utilizes porcelain as a sculptural canvas and often references the iconic teapot form and reconfigured vessel forms as a formal vehicle for narrative storytelling. The miniaturized scale of her relief sculptures and figurines allows her to survey their worlds as landscapes inhabited by her subjects, their surroundings embellished by her personal iconography, literal comments, and observations on the themes.

"Art is my entire life; it's just exactly what I gravitated toward. As a small child my grandfather was a butcher and would give me large sheets of butcher paper on which I would draw geisha dolls in pencil. They were elaborate with big hair, pins, kimonos, and it goes on and on."

As a young student, Mara was drawn in by the encyclopedic collection of art at the Metropolitan Art Museum, which she visited regularly. In college she was exposed to conceptual and traditional art, but it was the art history courses that opened up her world to narrative. After college she married her art professor, Roy Superior, which afforded her continued education in an

"The Pearl Fishers (detail)" c. 2014, 12"×16"×3". High fired slab built and sculpted porcelain, painted with ceramic underglazes and oxides. Wall relief sculpture.

academic community. "My entire life has been a life in art school; I wouldn't want any other life. I am the luckiest person."

After college she worked as a retail display artist. It was the most artistic position available. It wasn't until her husband accepted a teaching position at Hampshire College in Western, Massachusetts, that she took her first class to learn hand-building with porcelain. That class changed her life and prompted her to go to graduate school to focus exclusively on working with porcelain. One thing led to another when her husband's student, Leslie Ferrin, graduated and decided to open a studio in

"Tulipomania" c. 2011, 32"×24"×24". High fired slab built and sculpted porcelain sculpture, painted with ceramic underglazes and oxides.

Northampton. She secured a studio with retail space and was in business immediately following graduation. Leslie started selling work from local ceramic artists. Soon thereafter Mara and Barbara Walsh partnered with Leslie, and this is how the influential Pinch Pottery Gallery was established. Mara sold her work there and through craft shows, such as the Philadelphia Craft Show, which exposed her to the editors of the larger magazines such as *American Craft* and *Ceramics Monthly*. Mara sold her work through higher end craft shows for the first fifteen years and for the past fifteen years has been selling work through two galleries, one of which is Ferrin Contemporary Gallery.

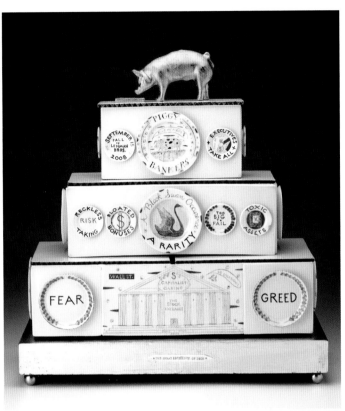

"Piggy Bankers" c. 2010, High fired, slab built porcelain sculpture, painted with ceramic underglazes and oxides.

The warm reception Mara received early on in her career by showing at craft fairs exposed her work to collectors and editors, but that aspect of the market has shifted for her. Mara states that craft shows are not what they used to be for all kinds of reasons, including demographics, economics, and generational differences.

"The younger generations are presenting themselves online, and they are doing it beautifully. I'm observing what the next generation is doing for marketing; it's brilliant! So the world has changed radically in thirty years."

Her most influential mentor has been her husband, Roy Superior. "I lived with a remarkable, renaissance professor—a brilliant man." With respect making a living, Mara admits, "It always helps if you are an artist for there to be one person with a steady income in the relationship, and that was my husband. So I had the great privilege of being able to be a studio artist…It would have been very rocky if I had to go out to work. I would be a terrible waitress. Roy always pushed me; he would say, 'Stop making the small

"The most important thing to me is getting my work into a museum. If I can get a piece of my work into the Metropolitan Museum, I can die and go to heaven happily; I have done my job."

stuff; make the best work of your life.' We were completely impractical people."

"It was lucky that I met my husband so young and he connected me with Leslie Ferrin, a visionary who started the gallery and the group studio with seven artists." Today Mara and Donna McGee are the only two artists left working out of the E Street Clay studio in Hadley, Massachusetts. She credits her professional relationship with Leslie as the luckiest business relationship of her career.

Her advice to graduating artists is "Put yourself in a community with other artists because the attrition rate is so huge. If you are not really encouraged to continue to work in a community, it is very easy to move out because it is so complicated."

Slow and steady, something wonderful can happen every day, like being published or having someone buy your work. But for David and Roberta Williamson, a wonderful creative jeweler duo, the small things are what make it all worth it. Roberta grew up in the Pilsen area of Chicago and remembers looking out of her window at a brick wall or walking outside to see a landscape devoid of vegetation. One day her father drove the family out to a house in the suburbs of the city that he had secretly built for them. "I remember jumping out of the car, and it was the first time I had ever heard birds, seen grass or trees, or smelled clean air. That was the exact moment I knew I was an artist. I just had a flood of stimulus and I started drawing and making things."

David and Roberta met during their freshman year at Northern Illinois University. Roberta was a fine metals major and David was a math major. "I started college with no goals and no plan; I was just trying to avoid going to Vietnam. I remember walking by the art building and looking through the window at what I thought was an archaeology lab with excavated objects. I brought Roberta over to talk her into taking [an archaeology] class with me, but she told me it was a ceramics class. I was so naïve! I was just so fascinated that you could make those things with your hands." They both feel that the world of creativity is just so breathtaking. David later transferred into the ceramics program, studying with Jack Earl.

David and Roberta Williamson

Mixed Media / Fine Metals

"The Third Person between Us: I" c. 2013, 18"×9"×1". Hand fabricated jewelry, metal and found objects. Sterling silver, copper, crystal, paper, vintage slate, wood, steel, glass.

"The Secret" 7"×14"×1". Hand fabricated jewelry, metal, and found objects. Sterling silver, copper, porcelain vintage French cameo, leaves, antique print, vintage slate, steel.

David and Roberta attribute much of their knowledge to the numerous wonderful professors they've both had. They learned to be humble and appreciate the small moments and successes, as well as learning the ins and outs of running a business as artists. "There was a little farm between the college and Chicago. Ever fall they would invite artists in the area to sell their work. Each artist had a card table, and you could admire the work and purchase it directly. The artists were phenomenal, like Ruth Duckworth and Don Reitz. That's how we learned how it's really done."

David and Roberta currently sell their work at the Philadelphia Craft Show, Smithsonian Craft Show, and the American Craft Expo in Evanston. Every piece they sell is a new connection between the maker and the buyer. They love hearing comments

"Cecropia" c. 2013, 22"×1.25"×.25". Necklace. Hand fabricated bezel set. Sterling silver, fine silver, quartz crystal, antique prints.

"Talking about commitment… the year we got married, we were trying to save money for graduate school, so we moved into my parents' attic. We had no tools and no studio. I worked during the day as a garbage man trying to earn as much money as possible. Roberta set up a little card table in the attic. She would collect sticks and twigs from the backyard that had nice markings and make jewelry just out of sticks. Her creative drive was still there, and that's what is so key, no matter what: she has to make."

and feedback about the work. "Every piece we make is precious and personal to us, so they're hard to part with. The people who have our work become our lifelong friends and have a very special place in our lives."

While David and Roberta are both very committed to their daily studio practice, they also have been teachers for forty years. Roberta is an adjunct jewelry teacher at Baldwin Wallace University, where David is a professor of art. Teaching has provided them with a steady income that helps finance their fair fees and materials. "Teaching has also held us back from our full potential. It's all consuming, but each of our students is like family." Although teaching is physically and emotionally exhausting, they feel that it ultimately adds to their relationships.

David and Roberta's studio is not what you would expect. They work publicly at a large table in the hallway of the university. They wheel carts out to work, and roll them away to lock them up when they are done working. Each piece they're working on has its own tray. As one of them finishes an element of a piece, they push the tray on across the table. Rotating through pieces allows David

David and Roberta. Image from LOOT, c. 2013, the Museum of Arts and Design, New York.

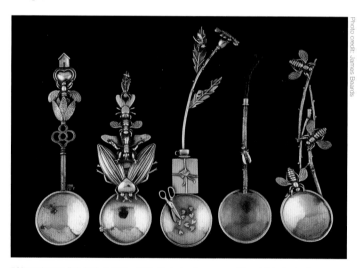

"Abundance." 6.25"×1.25"×.25". Group of spoons. Hand fabricated. Sterling silver.

and Roberta to always have a fresh set of eyes on the composition and the quality. "We are just so synchronized. It's a flow that works so well for us. We always say it's the third person between us that makes the work; we are just the facilitators." By working

"In Sycamore, the town holds a big dump day where you place all your unwanted items on the curb and the town hauls them away. On our first date we went garbage picking for objects… before we even knew what to do with them! We knew we were meant for each other."

"The Torn Paper" c. 2014, 3.5"×7.5". Hand fabricated and bezel set. Sterling silver, fine silver, copper, altered antique print, glass.

in public, they remain accessible to students, but this also allows students to see the commitment and passion that goes into being a successful artist.

In the last few years, David and Roberta have lent their collaborative skills to the corporate world, working for companies like Tide detergent. The duo talks to teams who are developing new products and works with them to facilitate a natural conversation about the spirit of collaborative enterprise. "You're trying to make a product as good as it can be. Sometimes, these teams are vastly different ages, or different departments, but the goal is always the same. We teach them to let their ego go."

"We have always put family first. There was a period of time when we were dealing with some aging family that pulled us away from making for a long time. We felt so discombobulated. When we got home, we went to the studio and looked at all of the work we'd made over the years and got tears in our eyes. This is really who we are." David and Roberta make their work mostly for personal satisfaction. They aren't consumed by a need to sell it

"The Queen" c. 2014, 3.5"×1.75"×.5". Brooch/pendant. Hand fabricated, sterling silver, brass, copper, watchmaker's crystal, antique print, vintage button.

Living room detail, c. 2015.

Living room detail, c. 2015.

but are interested more in the way people respond to it. Roberta says they consistently push each piece to the limit. Despite their work's conservative exterior, each piece embodies their wild spirits.

"Personal relationships are so important. They define all moments in a narrative way; the work just acts as a connector."

Sasha Zhitneva

Glass

sashazhitneva.com

Originally from Russia, Sasha Zhitneva is a designer and artist who began working in glass in 1995. She studied in Russia, Spain, and in the United States, where her artistic journey began at the age of forty. Primarily known for her own "signature style" abstract fused panels, Sasha has developed a diverse body of work in glass—ranging from stained, painted, laminated, cold and warm fused, and mosaics, including a line of kiln-formed jewelry. Aside from her gallery artwork, she has also completed a number of architectural and lighting installations in both stained glass and kiln-formed glass and, more recently, repurposed discarded plastic bottles and containers.

During her elementary education Sasha enjoyed traditional basic art training. She then continued on to take several courses

"Exodus Windows" c. 2003, 3'×15'. Stained glass panels, hand-painted, etched, laminated. The Jewish Fellowship of Hemlock Farms, Lords Valley, Pennsylvania.

"J, Fox & Blu" c. 2014. 13"×21". Multilayered laminated panel. Painted with glass enamels and glass frit. Fused and cast inclusions.

"When I finally embraced that path, it became my life and now it feels that it's the only one I've ever lived, even though I am well aware that's not true."

"Con Brio" c. 2008, 10"×18". Kiln-formed glass panel.

in graphic design and, as an adult, numerous techniques-based glass classes, as well as private classes with artists whose work she liked, "to get her started." Her development as an artist is mostly rooted in her exploration. "In large part, I am also

self-taught, as far as learning new software, keeping up with upgrades, and honing techniques I need for my artwork."

Sasha claims she was seduced by glass because of its beauty and the unlimited possibilities it offered to manipulate color, light, and shadows. Glass also draws her because it allows her to work in both two and three dimensions, using glass cane to create line drawing and sheet glass to create forms and depth.

Sasha is expanding the technique of glass lamination, or "cold fusing," by combining the functionality of modern architectural glazing substrates, insulate, and safety glass with the tradition of stained glass artistry. This allows her to expand the palette and the scale, which was previously technically constrained by the use of only traditional methods.

"I learned to admire glass's personality traits. It doesn't tarnish, the colors don't fade when exposed to sun, it keeps appearances till broken. Most importantly, its unstoppable capacity of reincarnation tops it all—broken, smashed, ground, and even entirely reduced to dust, glass could be placed into a kiln, re-fused, and it re-emerges as its new self."

Sasha finds herself to be most productive in her studio, located in her home, after 6 p.m. If she's having a hard time coming up with ideas, she will work freely on "nonsense" pieces to get the creative juices flowing, in addition to doing color and shape studies in preparation for larger pieces. When she gets an idea for a project she says that she "vividly remembers what came to mind and it stays there until I start working on it." She prefers not to use a sketchbook to fully work out ideas because, for her, in the process of working the project out on paper, the idea loses

> "I am an artist because it's my way of thinking things through—making art is like creating one's own language."

Sasha working on "skyPod."

vitality. If it lives in her imagination, she explains, she thinks about it and transforms the idea with any new insights that come to her as she works. Once she feels like bringing the idea to life, that's when the idea is alive and current. She may then do a few sketches to explore a direction, but rarely keeps them after the piece is finished.

Sasha moves freely between two- and three-dimensional methods to develop her ideas, working graphically as well as in a painterly way. She develops compositional complexities in her most recent works by combining traditional methods of constructing stained glass with cold lamination and painting on glass. And she incorporates new and recycled glass components, which are sometimes kiln fused before becoming part of a larger composition.

Her new work is rooted in raising awareness of our waste, and concerns for a sustainable future. The "reFused" series uses

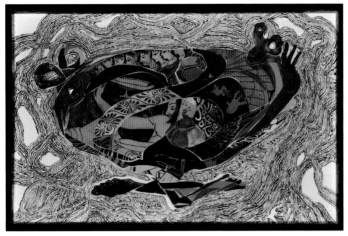

"Kylix" c. 2014. 18"×11". Multilayered laminated panel. Painted with glass enamels and glass frit. Cast glass inclusions.

"Coming Back as Another Being" 21"×17". Multilayered laminated panel with fused, slumped, and painted glass inclusions.

discarded materials such as water bottles, plastic bags, and plastic food containers to create compositions that are constructed or painted, altered, joined, exposed to heat, and more—exploring the possibilities within discarded materials in beautiful ways.

Sasha uses social media sparingly, but has utilized the networking aspects to connect with other artists to collaborate with. She says this has been a very rewarding way to work with peers. She sells her work through her website and galleries, and she teaches workshops at various glass centers and craft schools.

About the Authors

Jacklyn Scott was born into an artistic family and spent most of her childhood in her mother's clay studio, volunteering at craft centers, and working at Peters Valley School of Craft during college summers. Her exposure to the beauty of handmade objects and the interesting people who make them led her to study at the Tyler School of Art in Philadelphia, where she explored her many interests in printmaking, sculpture, and ceramics. She now works full time at Hood College in Frederick, Maryland, as the Studio Manager for the Art Department where she is currently working towards her MFA in Ceramic Arts. Jacklyn is eager to find and make her way as a professional artist.

Kristin Müller, artist and executive director at Peters Valley School of Craft, approaches all aspects of her work as a designer resourcefully and adaptively based on lessons learned along the way. Prior to establishing her studio in northeast Pennsylvania she wore many hats, working as a studio artist in New Haven, Connecticut, as adjunct faculty at three colleges, and as education director, curator, and ceramics instructor at Brookfield Craft Center. She wrote *The Potter's Studio Handbook: A Guide to Hand Built and Wheel-Thrown Ceramics* (Quarry) and recently completed an MFA in ceramics at Hood College, where she teaches in the graduate program. Her work is exhibited widely and her ceremonial tea bowls are held in private collections. Visit www.kristinmuller.com and www.petersvalley.org.

Tommy Simpson is an "imaginist" who works in nearly every medium, including woodworking, painting, printmaking, clay, woodcarving, bookmaking, jewelry, and even prose. In each work of art there is an identifiable style that "puzzles together" the artist's personal and cultural references into a signature blend of joyfulness and subtle commentary. "The ultimate goal," Tommy says, "is to bring the artwork to life, so that the viewer can identify the human spirit behind the work, and experience its poetry." Simpson's artwork is exhibited nationally, including at the Renwick Gallery at the American Art Museum at the Smithsonian Institute, Washington, DC; the Museum of Art and Design, New York; and the Boston Museum of Fine Arts. His work can be found in many collections worldwide.

Stuart Kestenbaum is former director of the Haystack Mountain School of Crafts in Deer Isle, and in 2016 was named poet laureate of Maine.